AND NOT MANY PEOPLE KNOW
THIS EITHER!

This follow-up to NOT MANY PEOPLE KNOW
THAT! is not to be missed. Hundreds more
indispensable facts about every topic under
the sun.

From murder: the secretary bird stamps its
victims to death
To music: Ravel composed only nineteen
hours in forty-two years

From love: snails kiss before mating
To London: the Great Fire only actually killed
six people

From politics: the original Tories were a band
of Irish outlaws
To palaces: Greenwich was the first to have
glass in its windows

If you are one of the thousands who told your
friends and family "Not many people know
that!", you'll relish this new collection.

**Also by the same author,
and available in Coronet Books:**

NOT MANY PEOPLE KNOW THAT!

About the Author

Born in 1933, the son of a Billingsgate fish
porter, Michael Caine was brought up in
Bermondsey in London's East End. He
attended school in Peckham. After a variety
of jobs, it was as office boy to a film producer
that he first became interested in acting.

He has appeared and starred in numerous
films, his first major triumph coming in 1963
with 'Zulu'. Many successful films followed,
including 'The Ipcress File', 'Alfie' (Oscar
nomination for Best Actor), 'California Suite',
'The Honorary Consul' and 'Educating Rita'
for which he won the British Academy Award
for Best Actor.

Michael Caine lives in Los Angeles,
California, with his wife, Shakira, and two
daughters. He frequently visits Britain.

And Not Many People Know This Either!

Michael Caine's Second
Collection of Amazing
Information

Illustrations by John Jensen

**Royalties to the National
Playing Fields Association**

CORONET BOOKS
Hodder and Stoughton

Text copyright © 1985 Michael Caine

Illustrations copyright © 1985 John Jensen

First published in Great Britain in 1985 by
Robson Books Ltd

Coronet edition 1986
Second impression 1986

British Library C.I.P.

Caine, Michael
   And not many people know this either!:
Michael Caine's second collection of
amazing information
   1. Curiosities and wonders
   I. Title
032'.02   AG243

ISBN 0–340–39982–1

Printed and bound in Great Britain for
Hodder and Stoughton Paperbacks, a
division of Hodder and Stoughton Ltd.,
Mill Road, Dunton Green, Sevenoaks,
Kent (Editorial Office: 47 Bedford
Square, London, WC1B 3DP) by
Cox & Wyman Ltd., Reading.

Introduction

Acting in films has a lot in common with collecting oddball facts and scraps of information. You shoot in tiny sections; the script is dissected into morsels for each scene; for a few brief minutes (sometimes just seconds) your energy is channelled into one fragment of the film before being directed right away into another. The common element linking the two is concentration.

As a film actor I've had to train my mind to zero in on individual scenes like a laser. It may not be the most powerful of minds, but it has the advantage over some I can think of of being able to target straight in on to the object of attention. So it is with collecting information – I've only to hear something that interests me raised in a conversation, and I find my mind homing in on this and scooping it up to be stored away for future use.

Being in the Army had its part to play, too. When I was called up for my National Service, I got myself in with a right bunch – they were always getting into arguments, and always getting their facts wrong. So I soon found myself acting as an arbiter, and constantly correcting my mates, until it got to the stage when almost every argument ended with someone saying, 'All right, then, we'll go and ask Mick.'

Having a retentive memory is handy, too, when it comes to developing a part in a film (or a play for that matter). I've got a sort of mental card index of people I've either seen or met, which I 'flick' through until I find what I'm looking for. It's like fishing. Once the character is hooked there's no losing him, and I'm lucky in being able to switch the character I'm playing on and off like a lightbulb. It's the same as plucking a gobbet of information out of the air and then forgetting about it until it's needed the next time.

I've also realized it's very important to have interests right outside my work. My house, the garden, painting, good restaurants, are just some of the important elements that help me to unwind – the one thing that's never discussed *chez Caine* is the film industry! That's why I've decided to use film titles here to act as 'coat-hangers' for this second collection of nuggets of amazing information. As I think is the case in my own life, the films I've chosen act as points of departure into a wider and infinitely more intriguing world outside.

I hope you agree.

And Not Many People Know This Either!

The First Time

Orville Wright who, with his brother, was the first man to fly, was also involved in the world's first fatal aircrash.

The first authenticated British earthquake occurred in AD 974.

Thanks to satellite photos, the dark side of the moon was seen for the first time in 1959.

Roscoe 'Fatty' Arbuckle, the first million-dollar movie star, was also the first to be banned from the screens.

The world's first doughnut-hole machine was patented in 1872, the same year that the first toothpick machine was introduced.

The Swedish were the first nation to scrap glass milk bottles in favour of paper cartons.

The first recorded operation for varicose veins was performed on the Roman consul Marius (155-86 BC). It was so painful that he had only one leg done.

The first bathtub in America was owned by Benjamin Franklin.

The first magician to saw a woman in half was Count de Grisley in 1799.

Queen Elizabeth I owned the first wristwatch.

The first pair of false eyelashes was developed in Hollywood. It was made of human hair woven into tiny strips of cloth and stuck on to the eyelid.

The earliest evidence of cancer was discovered in Java ape-man, found in 1891 and believed to be half a million years old.

The first newspaper headline was on the front page of the *New York Gazette* in 1777.

Giraffes used to be known as camelopards.

The first American hat factory produced eighteen hats a week.

* *The First Time* was a 1968 'first love' comedy. It starred Jacqueline Bisset, who went on to star in *Inchon* (1982), a movie masterminded and financed by Sun Myung Moon of Moonie fame. *Inchon* has gone down in movie history as a classic disaster. Not only was it expensive — Bisset alone received $1.65 million — but in one scene in which Sir Laurence Olivier plays General MacArthur his trousers change colour three times.

What A Way To Go

Anne Boleyn was buried in a box that had contained arrows; no one had thought to provide a coffin for her.

Molière died on stage while acting the role of an invalid in *Le Malade Imaginaire*, a play he had written himself.

In the nineteenth century in Britain, failed suicides were hanged.

Pope John XII was beaten to death by a furious husband who found the pontiff making love to his wife.

Two players died during the Army Cup Final football match in front of the King and Queen in 1948.

When the bearded vulture is hungry and can't find any dead prey, it knocks suitable victims off cliffs.

In 1936 a Bavarian publican died after being bitten in the neck by one of his customers.

Oracio Pucci had the doubtful distinction of being hanged from the very same bar of the very same window of the Palazzo Vecchio from which his father had been hanged — and by the same person, Francesco I.

Sir Arthur Aston, a Royalist commander during the Civil War, was beaten to death with his own wooden leg by Cromwell's troops.

A thirteenth-century English baron, Fitzwaine Fulk, was suffocated inside his armour when his horse became stuck in a bog.

Attila the Hun is said to have died while making love.

Christine Chubbock, a newsreader for an American TV station, shot herself in front of the cameras. When her script was checked, it was discovered that she had allowed time in the schedule for her suicide.

In 1938, Miss Phyllis Newcombe spontaneously combusted while waltzing in a dance hall crowded with onlookers.

* *What a Way to Go* was a 1963 black comedy starring Shirley MacLaine, Dick Van Dyke, Gene Kelly, Robert Mitchum and Paul Newman. Not many people know that Robert Mitchum composed the music for two songs in *Thunder Road*, made in 1958.

The Best of Enemies

At full tilt a rabbit can run at 34 mph. A fox can achieve only 27 mph.

The carnivorous bladderwort plant is the male flea's enemy. It looks just like a female flea, but when he jumps on it, it traps and digests him.

During the nineteenth century, Turkey suffered 13 military defeats and won only one campaign.

During World War II, more than 56,000 carrier pigeons went into action; some of them even won bravery awards.

Henrik Ibsen, the famous Norwegian dramatist, insisted on having a picture of his arch-rival August Strindberg over his desk to make him work harder.

In 1888, a football match to decide the Champions of the World was played between English Cup winners West Bromwich Albion and a Scottish club, Renton, winners of the Scottish Cup. Renton won.

Handel fought a duel with a conductor over who should conduct an opera.

Some moths send out jamming signals to confuse bats' high-frequency sound waves.

Car owners have a new enemy to look out for. The plastic components of car engines smell like female polecats, which is why an increasing number of male polecats are climbing under bonnets and gnawing through wiring and hoses.

When a new monarch takes the throne, he damages the Seal of his predecessor with a hammer.

The first cricket match to be held between two countries was between Canada and the USA in 1884.

King Boris of Bulgaria and his brother were both railway enthusiasts. They used to quarrel in public about who should drive the train they were travelling on.

In New York and San Francisco AIDS is the most common disease-related cause of death among young men.

* *The Best of Enemies*, starring David Niven, was a 1961 satirical comedy set in World War II. Niven's first name was originally James.

Tall Story

Lewis Carroll wrote his books while standing up.

The great European cathedrals were so solidly constructed that there is sometimes as much stone below ground as there is above it.

Because steel expands when it gets hot, the Eiffel Tower is 15 cm (6 inches) taller in summer than in winter.

A giraffe's blood pressure is at least twice that of a healthy man.

Tens of thousands of Ugandans reported that they had seen and heard a talking tortoise in 1978.

The Pyramids of Egypt are 5 km (3 miles) to the south of the point where they were originally built because the landmass has shifted since their construction.

Elephants really do have long memories, and the saying 'elephants never forget' may well be true.

A 1938 western, *The Terror of Tiny Town*, featured a cast of midgets riding Shetland ponies.

Blood is only slightly thicker than water.

The koala bear isn't a bear at all. It's a marsupial.

Dry ice doesn't melt. It evaporates.

There are approximately seven million tonnes of Epsom salts in every cubic mile (4.16 cubic kilometres) of sea water.

'Bluestocking', a term sometimes used to describe academic women, was originally applied to men who were members of a London literary club distinguished by its blue hose.

❝ I once experienced the awful truth at Cary Grant's house in Hollywood when I was trying to explain to him where my own house is. "You can't actually see it," I said, "but it's near those trees. It was built by a woman called Barbara Hutton for her son's twenty-first birthday present. She was the Woolworth heiress..." "Michael," Cary said, "you're talking about my stepson and my ex-wife, so don't explain who they are." ❞

* **The Awful Truth** was a hit comedy of 1937 starring Cary Grant and Irene Dunne. Not many people remember that it was Cary Grant who received Mae West's famous invitation in *She Done Him Wrong* (1933) — 'Why don't you come up sometime, see me?'

As You Like It

King George VI enjoyed sewing and once made a dozen embroidered chair covers.

All the members of the 20,000 Club have had sex in an aeroplane at more than 20,000 feet.

Some tribes of Papua New Guinea smoke their dead and preserve the remains.

The French eat more cheese per head each year than any other nation.

Philosopher Jeremy Bentham was fond of his unusual pet — a teapot.

George Washington carried a portable sundial for telling the time.

The Basenji, a species of dog from the Congo, cannot bark. It makes a yodelling noise and washes itself like a cat.

The Sepik crocodile likes to be a bit different; that's why its eggs are oblong and have white yolks.

The Romans were so keen on bathing that at the height of the Roman Empire they were each using 1,350 litres (300 gallons) of water a day.

The Great Gatsby might not have been liked by so many people had it been published under its original title — *Incident at West Egg*.

For their honeymoon, Beatrice and Sidney Webb went to Dublin to study trades unions.

The Chinese are wild about stamp-collecting.

Connoisseurs of possum meat say that it tastes just like veal.

Frederick the Great of Prussia used to drink coffee made with champagne.

Marie Antoinette and Louis XVI did not consummate their marriage until seven years after their wedding.

' Every time Greta Garbo's name is mentioned in Los Angeles somebody is sure to chime in with, 'Do you know she owns Rodeo Drive.' I always think there can't be many people who don't know that — not even Garbo! '

*   The 1936 film of *As You Like It* was adapted by J.M. Barrie, author of *Peter Pan*, and starred Laurence Olivier. Olivier once failed a screen test with Greta Garbo — though film legend has it that Garbo deliberately sabotaged it so that her lover John Gilbert would get the part.

The Awful Truth

James Cagney never uttered the immortal line, 'You dirty rat,' in any of his screen roles.

Princess Anne drives a car with a number plate that was originally on an Ealing milkfloat.

D.H. Lawrence, famed for his erotic novels, was actually a prude and would make love only in the dark.

Over the last decade, Thailand and Turkey have produced more films than the UK.

The original Tories were a band of Irish outlaws.

Charles Darwin did not actually talk about the 'survival of the fittest.'

The pig is reckoned by scientists to be the tenth most intelligent animal in the world.

Bulls are colour-blind. Matadors' cloaks are red to hide bloodstains, not to rouse the bull.

When scientists first started to put together the dinosaur fossils they'd found, they got them wrong. For many years the iguanodon was exhibited on all fours with its thumb sticking out of its forehead like a horn.

The ancient Swedes practised euthanasia by putting their old people into earthenware jars and leaving them there to die.

When H.G. Wells's *War of the Worlds* was broadcast, it was so realistic that a woman tried to poison herself rather than face attack by Martians. Two people were treated for heart attacks, and dozens went to hospital suffering fron shock.

Although Falabella horses are only 60 cm (24 in) high, they can run so fast that, over a short distance, they can beat a full-sized racehorse.

Termite hills measuring up to 6 m (20 ft) high have been found in Australia. Translated to the human scale, such hills would be four times the height of the Empire State Building.

'I made Hurry Sundown with Jane Fonda in the mid-sixties, a time when she was still seen as Hollywood's glamour starlet and I remember the surprise I had at finding a brilliant actress lurking there, waiting to emerge.'

* Jane Fonda was the female lead of *Tall Story*, made in 1960. In 1978, she and co-star Jon Voigt won Best Actress and Best Actor awards for their performances in the film *Coming Home*.

Bananas

For several centuries, women used to rub crushed strawberries on their breasts in the belief that it would enlarge them.

The world's longest banana split used more than 11,000 bananas and stretched for more than a mile (1.6 km).

Some bamboos can grow as much as a metre a day.

Don't eat buttercups — they can cause nasty indigestion.

Lemons and strawberries do not ripen after picking. Avocados and bananas do.

The seeds of the *coco-de-mer* tree resemble the female pelvis — and the tree is found only in one Seychelles island.

Milk from young coconuts was successfully used as blood plasma during World War II.

Saffron is made from the stamen of the crocus.

Study of a Finnish pine tree's roots has shown that they extend for 49 km (30 miles).

The durian fruit is an Asian delicacy. Unfortunately, it smells like the flesh of rotting corpses.

The bright red berries of the cuckoo-pint are poisonous to all creatures except the thrush.

Birch is the main constituent of plywood.

The first experiments in genetics involved garden peas.

Tonga once issued a postage stamp shaped like a banana.

Anyone who felled a hazel or apple tree was sentenced to death in ancient Ireland, where these trees were considered sacred.

* When Woody Allen was asked why he had called his 1971 comedy *Bananas* he replied that it was 'Because there are no bananas in it.'

Heaven Can Wait

There is no biblical authority for supposing that Christ's feet were nailed to the cross.

Joseph Stalin, who abolished religion in the USSR, trained for five years to be a priest.

The composer Franz Liszt took Catholic orders at the end of his life and requested that he be buried in his cassock with a requiem mass. He had the bad fortune to die during the Wagner festival at Bayreuth and, everyone being busy, was quickly laid to rest by a Protestant clergyman without any ceremony.

Psalm 117, verse 2, is the middle, in terms of the number of words, of the Bible.

Miss Piggy, star of the *Muppet Show*, was removed from Turkish TV during religious festivals so that viewers wouldn't be offended by the sight of an 'unclean' animal.

The people of Jordan are prepared to wait for heaven — Jordan has the lowest suicide rate in the world.

Alexander the Great's body was kept preserved in a jar of honey.

Major Peter Labellaire was so disenchanted with the 'topsy-turvy' world that he asked to be buried head downwards to see if he could make more sense of things.

In 1542 God's wig and tunic cost a shilling — as provided by the costume-maker for the Coventry Mystery Play.

An eleventh-century Benedictine monk called Oliver of Malmesbury decided that he couldn't wait until he was heaven-bound for his wings, so he built his own and tried to fly from the top of a high tower. Neither faith nor engineering kept him from an early reunion with his maker.

During the fifteenth century, men and women were segregated in church, being made to sit on either side of the aisle.

6 *Warren and I were in Mayfair once, looking at girls' backs and making bets whether they'd be beautiful or not when we got round to the front. We noticed one buying a newspaper, made the bet, tapped her on the shoulder and found she was Candice Bergen. It was Warren which won!* 9

*   The 1978 version of *Heaven Can Wait* starred Warren Beatty, who also wrote and directed it. Despite his notorious affairs and flings, Beatty is still one of America's most eligible bachelors.

Another Country

Bulgaria has the biggest rose
gardens in the world; from them
comes attar of roses, an oil which
forms the basis of many perfumes.

St George is the patron saint of Portugal as well as
England.

The world's shortest frontier is that
dividing Spain and Gibraltar.

All the gold for British royal wedding rings is mined
at Golgau in Wales.

The national flower of Sweden is the
lily of the valley.

The Chinese were eating rhubarb in 3,000 BC.

The government of Dubai has bought a
snowplough — to shift sand off the
roads.

845 dialects are spoken in India.

The first recorded Venetian gondolas
appeared in 1094.

Nowhere in France is more than 500 km (310 miles)
from the sea.

King Minos's palace on Crete was built in 2,000 BC, yet it has 'modern' plumbing, including running water and toilets.

In 1956, the Olympic equestrian sports had to be held in Stockholm while all the other events went on in Melbourne, Australia. This was because of the strict Australian quarantine laws.

Canada has the longest coastline in the world.

In France April Fool's Day is known as Fish Day.

Icelandic women don't change their names on marriage, and family members have different surnames with boys' names following their father's and girls' their mother's.

Trinidad has the world's largest asphalt lake and exports asphalt for surfacing roads all over the world.

* Based on the public-school years of Soviet spy Guy Burgess, *Another Country* (1984) disappointed some of its viewers because of the mildness of its sex scenes. It probably didn't go down well in the Bible Belt of the USA, which has the highest concentration of sex cinemas in the country — even more than in permissive California!

Murder By Death

Statistics indicate that more murderers come from Yorkshire than any other English county.

Henry VI's murder at the Tower of London in 1471 is commemorated each year by representatives of the educational establishments he founded — King's College, Cambridge and Eton. Roses and lilies are laid at the spot where he died.

Two American tramps died in 1903, apparently of cleanliness. They were given their first bath for twenty years and scrubbed down with a broom, an experience which proved too much for them.

The fate of Manichaeus indicates the problems the earliest doctors faced. When he failed to cure a Persian king's son, he was skinned alive and fed to the dogs.

Having murdered her employer, housekeeper Kate Webster made as much profit as possible out of her by selling her false teeth and rendering the body down to make dripping.

Al Llegas, a fighting-cock trainer, died when one of his birds turned on him and stabbed him to death with its razor-sharp spurs.

An attempt was made to kill a fifteenth-century pope by sending him papers contaminated with plague germs.

Napoleon may have been poisoned by his wallpaper. Copper arsenite, which can be poisonous, was used in the green pigment in nineteenth-century wallpaper, and Napoleon's room on St Helena was decorated with green paper.

The secretary bird stamps its victims to death.

In 1808 two Frenchmen fought a pistol duel — in hot air balloons suspended over Paris. One man missed his shot but the other was more accurate and watched his opponent plummet more than a thousand feet to his death.

I once gave a party on location and sat Glenda Jackson next to David Niven. Inside ten minutes the self-possessed, even formidable, actress had been reduced to a teenage film fan. The Niven charm was always devastating, and Glenda had a wonderful evening.

*   *Murder by Death* (1976), was an all-star extravaganza, a spoof murder mystery featuring Maggie Smith, David Niven, Alec Guinness, Peter Sellers and Truman Capote. Niven, who made his name as the archetypal English gentleman, first appeared on film as a Mexican in a blanket.

Everything You Always Wanted To Know About Sex

The Chinese didn't kiss until the practice was introduced by westerners, and they're still not very keen on it.

A worldwide survey of men's tastes in women revealed that plump women were more in demand than slim ones.

Flatworms sometimes reproduce by pulling themselves apart. Each part develops into a worm.

The Amazons believed that lame men made the best lovers and consequently used to break the legs of their male captives.

During the rutting season deer's antlers become highly erogenous.

The oldest sex manuals were published in China 5,000 years ago.

Some single cells have no fewer than eight different sexes.

Mink and sable hold the record for the longest mating. Times of up to eight hours have been recorded.

Oysters change sex according to the temperature of the water around them.

Wild cabbage was traditionally recommended as an aphrodisiac.

According to a survey, the second most popular reason for having sex is to produce a baby.

Homosexuality is illegal in 23 states in the USA.

Before mating, earthworms produce a special mucus to glue themselves together.

* *Everything You Always Wanted to Know About Sex* was Woody Allen's 1972 film tribute to the sex manual. One of the earliest sex films of all was *The Flea*, made in 1896, in which a girl infested with a flea takes her clothes off in the search for it.

The Adventurer

Prince Charles is the first heir to the throne to ride on the back of a killer whale.

W. Somerset Maugham was sent as an agent to Russia in 1917 but failed in his mission, partly because his stammer made the transmission of secret messages difficult.

Sir Richard Burton, celebrated English adventurer, wanted to enter Mecca where only Muslims are allowed. Not only did he dress up as an Arab, but he had himself circumcised for the occasion.

President Lyndon B. Johnson ran away from home at the age of 15 and didn't go back for two years.

During his famous game of golf on the moon, Alan Shepherd used a six iron.

In 1976 a South American guppy became the first fish in space.

T.E. Lawrence, known as Lawrence of Arabia, used a fleet of Rolls Royces to transport his unit when he led British forces against the Turks in Syria.

Casanova, renowned as the world's greatest lover, details only 132 conquests in his autobiography. Even allowing for those women he left out, he had far fewer lovers than Sarah Bernhardt, Brigitte Bardot and Napoleon, to name but a few.

When Magellan crossed the Pacific
Ocean, he was lucky enough not to
encounter a storm — hence his name
for the ocean. In fact the Pacific has
some of the roughest storms in the
world.

Dante, Christopher Marlowe, Daniel Defoe, Andrew
Marvell and Lord Byron all acted as government
spies.

The sooty tern is on the wing for as
long as three years before it returns to
its nesting grounds.

Dr James Barry qualified as a doctor, enlisted in the
army and became an Inspector-General. It was only
on 'his' death in 1865 that 'he' was discovered to be
a woman.

❛ Charlie Chaplin was born next to the Kennington Granada,
not far from where I was brought up. On a visit home I went
to look round the old neighbourhood and bumped into him
doing the same thing. What's more we met up there three
years later, making another trip down memory lane.❜

* ***The Adventurer*** was one of Charlie
Chaplin's early knockabout comedies. He
wrote, directed and starred in it in 1917.
More books have been written about the
life and art of Chaplin than about any
other screen star.

Anything Goes

Investigations into Post Office reliability have revealed that Tuesday is the best day to post an urgent letter. More first class letters arrive at their destinations on Wednesday than letters posted on any other day of the week.

In 1970 a New Zealand driver drove backwards for 175 km (109 miles).

Charles Darwin suffered from terrible fainting fits.

Chippendale worked mainly in mahogany.

Only about one third of the world's population eats with a knife and fork.

Crocodile tail steaks are said to taste like lobster.

London University was the first to permit women to take degrees.

The ruby is currently the world's most precious gem.

King Olav V of Norway is 37th in line of succession to the English throne.

On average, a tin can will disintegrate in 100 years.

The average flying speed for a butterfly is about 32 km/h (20 mph).

Wallpaper first became popular in England in the 1720s.

Cricket pads were invented in 1836.

King Richard II suffered from *anorexia nervosa*.

The distance a cow's moo travelled was used as a unit of measurement in India for 2,000 years.

More than half a million cars are stolen annually in Great Britain.

Until the sixteenth century men did not wear underwear.

Mae West wrote a play simply entitled *Sex*.

* *Anything Goes*, a musical comedy with music by Cole Porter, has been filmed twice, in 1936 and 1956. Bing Crosby had the distinction of having starred in both versions.

Ain't Misbehavin'

On early railway journeys ladies held pins between their lips while travelling through dark tunnels, just in case gentlemen took advantage of the gloom and kissed them.

In Tibet, the traditional greeting is a low bow followed by sticking the tongue out three times.

Edwardian ladies were warned never to speak to a man smoking a cigar. If they did, he would have to throw it away — and cigars were expensive.

Shoulder pads were considered shocking and vain in the fifteenth century, though no one seemed to mind the outrageous codpieces that were all the rage among men.

Victorian ladies paying calls on each other were instructed to stay fifteen minutes — not a moment more nor less. Difficult when they were also forbidden to look at a clock or watch...

Prince Philip, who does not enjoy horse racing, is rumoured to conceal a transistor radio in his top hat at Ascot so that he can listen to the cricket results.

Victorian ladies were advised never to place books by male and female authors next to each other on their library shelves unless the authors were married.

The correct way to eat curry is with a spoon and fork. Jelly should be eaten with a fork alone, according to etiquette books.

The Queen does not have to pay income tax, nor does she have to put stamps on her letters.

Throughout the seventeenth and eighteenth centuries most people carried their own sets of cutlery because hosts did not provide knives and forks for guests.

Crocodiles cannot stick out their tongues.

Courtiers at Versailles grew the little fingernails of their left hands so that they could use them for scratching on doors — it was considered rude to knock.

Masai warriors consider it a sign of politeness to spit at each other.

*   *Ain't Misbehavin'*, made in 1955, was an American version of *Pygmalion* with music — in some ways a forerunner of *My Fair Lady*.

Accident

One of the world's stickiest accidents occurred in Boston in the US when a giant tank containing two million gallons of molasses burst and flooded part of the city. Twenty-one people were killed, many of them drowned in treacle.

To avoid accidents on the day of her coronation, the Queen wore her crown for several days beforehand and accustomed herself to its weight.

A Spanish Air Force jet shot itself out of the sky when its gunfire ricochetted off a nearby mountainside.

The only Englishman to become Pope, Nicholas Breakspear, died after choking on a fly he'd accidentally swallowed.

According to accident reports, the chance of being killed in an air crash is smaller than that of being kicked to death by a donkey.

In northern India in 1888, 246 people were killed by hail.

Thomas Carlyle, eminent Victorian writer, sent the manuscript of his *History of the French Revolution* to his friend John Stuart Mill to read. Mill's maid burned it, mistaking it for waste paper. There was no copy.

An American man was electrocuted when he urinated on a live railway line in the New York subway.

Allan Pinkerton, founder of the famous detective agency, died of gangrene after tripping and biting his tongue.

The worst plane crash in the world happened on the ground.

The diarist Samuel Pepys was accidentally made sterile by an operation to remove his gallstones.

An eighteenth-century English eccentric tried to cure his hiccups by setting light to his night shirt. It is not recorded whether the cure worked.

'It was Stanley Baker, as a producer three years before his appearance in Accident, who gave me my first big break in Zulu.'

* Accident was an all-British production of 1967. It starred Dirk Bogarde, who had also featured in the first British film to confront seriously the problems of homosexuality. Victim, released in 1961, even went as far as having the word 'homosexual' in its dialogue.

All About Eve

Women are twice as likely as men to play bingo, but only half as likely to do the pools.

Mrs Beeton, famed for her book on household management, died at the age of 28.

Although it is generally believed that the female species is smaller than the male, most female insects are larger — and there are more insects in the world than all other creatures together.

Mary Queen of Scots owned one of the world's first billiard tables.

The court of the king of Siam was run entirely by women. Even the palace guards were female.

The first Duchess of Marlborough economized on ink by not dotting her i's or using full stops.

If beauty is only skin deep then in some places it's less than ½ mm (.013 inch) deep.

Catherine de Medici ordered that all women at the French court should have waists measuring no more than 22 cm (13 inches).

Many African queens kept all-male harems.

Caroline, wife of George IV, used to ride around with a pumpkin on her head to keep her cool.

Women are more sensitive to body language than men. They know what is wrong with a baby, for example, by its cry and gestures. Men have no idea.

Nell Gwynne called Charles II 'Charles the Third' because she'd already had two lovers called Charles.

Xhosa women of South Africa are permitted to smoke a pipe when they come of age.

Noah's wife is mentioned five times in the Bible, yet she is never named.

❛ I first met Bette Davis at a party I gave at the top of the Time-Life Building in New York. She told me I had a look of Leslie Howard, so I invited her out to dinner. "I'll come on one condition," she said, "I'm going home alone in the cab. You're not seeing me back!" ❜

* *All About Eve* (1950), won four Oscars and starred the wonderfully bitchy Bette Davis. Visitors to Boston's Museum of Fine Arts can see Ms Davis in the nude; at the age of 16, she posed naked for a statue of the goddess Diana, which is on exhibition there.

All Creatures Great and Small

Giraffes can lick their own ears.

The fish-eating bat of Central Africa scoops fish out of the water using the web between its legs.

The tuatara, a New Zealand reptile, can hold its breath for over an hour.

Dormice hibernate for six months of the year.

Chimpanzees have more chromosomes than humans.

Crocodiles and alligators are the noisiest reptiles.

Ants are capable of moving loads ten times their own weight.

Sepia was originally the name of the ink that is derived from the cuttlefish.

Earthworms are blind.

Lobsters have eight legs.

The ovaries of the barnacle are in its head.

Scientists have shown that by decapitating a caterpillar — which does not kill it — they can produce a headless butterfly which lives longer than a normal one because of its restricted life.

40 per cent of all mammals are rodents.

Nearly half the world's 8,580 species of bird migrate.

Polar bears flip fish out of the water with their paws.

Crocodiles can't chew. They seize part of their prey between their jaws and twist a piece off by spinning around in the water.

The silkworm moth has eleven brains.

Red squirrels attract more fleas than other animals.

* *All Creatures Great and Small*, which was released in 1974, was developed from the popular television programmes based on James Herriot's books.

Foul Play

In 1973 two blind teams of Peruvian footballers played a match using a ball filled with dried peas.

In AD 392 the Roman Emperor Theodosius cancelled future ancient Olympic Games after the 293rd Olympiad had ended in riots and arson.

1966 didn't start too well for Chester's football club. During a New Year's Day game both full backs had to leave the field with broken legs.

There are sixteen feathers on the standard badminton shuttlecock.

The first modern Olympic Games, held in Athens in 1896, were so disorganised that few countries bothered to send teams. The British team included sporting members of the local embassy and an Irishman who just happened to be on holiday. He won the gold medal for singles tennis.

The Aztecs used to play an ancient form of basketball.

Monaco's main revenue comes from its gambling casinos.

Joe Davis, legendary snooker champion, had only one eye.

The Turks are fans of the sport of camel wrestling.

Lieutenant Wyndham Halswelle won the 400 metre sprint at the London Olympics in 1908. In fact, he couldn't have come second if he'd tried, because he was the only man in the race, his opponents having withdrawn after being accused of cheating.

When in 1976 a Pakistani cricket umpire gave a number of controversial decisions against the fielding team, players pulled up the wicket and beat him to death with the stumps.

The Greek who won the marathon in the 1896 Olympics won not just a gold medal but also 365 meals and the hand of a millionaire's daughter in marriage. The last he had to forgo — he was already married.

❝ *Dudley Moore played his first film part with me in* The Wrong Box.❞

* *Foul Play* was a moderately well-received 1978 thriller starring Dudley Moore and Goldie Hawn. Dudley Moore and Mickey Rooney share the distinction of being the film world's shortest leading men; they are 1.6 metres (5 ft 3 in) tall.

All That Money Can Buy

Westminster Council spends more than £2 million each year on its public toilets.

On hearing the news of Prince Charles's birth, the people of America sent a gift of one-and-a-half tons of nappies to the Queen.

In the nineteenth century aluminium was more expensive than gold.

In the seventeenth century more money was spent on candles for the royal palaces than on food.

The cash register was invented in 1884.

Tea was once used as currency in Siberia.

Tutankhamun's inner coffin is the largest single gold object in the world.

British land prices have risen so high that a farmer who owns 250 acres is likely to be worth a million.

Howard Hughes's chauffeurs were instructed to drive in the middle of the road so that the car tyres didn't get covered in leaves and rubbish from the gutters.

Peggy Hopkins Joyce became one of the world's richest women by marrying five millionaires.

Hitler's Mercedes-Benz cars did only three miles to the gallon because they were so heavily armoured.

Slot machines were introduced for dispensing holy water around 100 BC.

The groat, a unit of English currency established in 1351, was not discontinued until 1856.

The Queen's milk is delivered in special bottles with her monogram on them.

In 1981 the cost of failed tests to would-be drivers was £13 million.

* *All That Money Can Buy* (1941) was released under three other titles as well. It starred Walter Huston, who in 1947 won an Oscar for Best Supporting Actor — the same year that his son John won *his* Oscar for Best Director.

Adam's Rib

Mary Queen of Scots was a member of the earliest golf club, St Andrew's, which was founded in 1552. She was probably the first woman golfer.

Cleopatra wrote treatises on cosmetics, weights and measures and coins.

Despite the efforts of Amelia Bloomer to popularize trousers for women, it wasn't until Marlene Dietrich wore trousers in a film with lesbian overtones that they really caught on.

Lillie Langtry became one of the first personalities to endorse a product when she appeared in advertisements for Pears soap.

Queen Victoria had to propose to Albert because protocol would not permit him to propose to her. It is not known whether our current queen had to propose to Prince Philip.

Finland had the first female MPs.

Marie Curie and her daughter received three Nobel prizes between them.

The first person to go over Niagara Falls in a barrel was a woman. She survived.

The most popular person in history, according to a 1976 survey at Madame Tussaud's, was Joan of Arc.

A Frenchwoman born in 1869 had two pelvises and four legs. Despite the handicap, she married and had two healthy children.

Mrs Ida Maitland had a bust measurement of 386 cm (152 in).

Barbara Cartland, queen of romance, was mainly responsible for the issuing of silk cami-knickers to women in the Forces in World War II.

Olga Korbut, the Soviet gymnast, was the first person in the world to do a backward somersault on the parallel bars.

❛ *If my acting can be said to be modelled on any one actor it's Spencer Tracy, and if I can make any single claim for its success it's that I once got a fan letter from Katharine Hepburn's sister!* ❜

* *Adam's Rib* paired Katharine Hepburn and Spencer Tracy in a brilliant 1949 comedy of the sexes. During his acting career Tracy received nine Oscar nominations, a feat equalled only by Laurence Olivier.

English Without Tears

The word 'nark', meaning a police spy, originated from the Romany word *nak*, meaning nose.

Food was known from the seventeenth century to the nineteenth as *bellytimber*.

There are about 600 slang English words to describe the penis.

The word 'love', used to mean zero in a tennis match, is derived from the French 'l'oeuf', meaning egg, because a written zero looks like an egg.

The word LASER is derived from the initial letters of Light Amplification by the Stimulated Emission of Radiation.

Italic type was invented in 1500.

The correct name for mother of pearl is nacre.

In Pidgin English, Prince Charles is *'Number one fellah belong missus Queen.'*

Shakespeare was the first person to use the words *bump, auspicious* and *critic*.

There have been 250 known alphabets but only 50 of them survive.

Translated into English, Hong Kong means 'fragrant harbour'.

The letters J and V were introduced into the English language around 1630.

Homonyms are words which sound identical but have different senses.

George Bernard Shaw backed the idea of phonetic spelling and a new alphabet, and he left money in his will to aid the cause.

The study of the quantities in which drugs should be administered is called posology.

Bristol was originally known as Brigstowe.

* *English Without Tears*, made in 1944, was a World War II comedy starring Margaret Rutherford, who is most famous for her role as Agatha Christie's sleuth, Miss Marple.

Never A Dull Moment

An acre of pasture can contain more than three million worms.

Recent surveys of library shelves have brought to light titles such as *Fun with Knotting String, Play With Your Own Marbles, How to Boil Water in a Paper Bag,* and *The Book of Marmalade, its Antecedents, History and Role in the World Today.*

Sir Christopher Cockerell's first hovercraft was made out of an old vacuum cleaner and a treacle tin.

The highest recorded number of faints at a royal occasion occurred during the funeral of George V. Three million people turned out to watch the procession and 15,000 of them fainted.

Paper was invented by a Chinese eunuch.

On their flight across the Atlantic, Alcock and Brown carried with them two stuffed cats.

The first European glass mirrors were produced in Venice in the 1300s.

In old English time a moment was either one-fortieth or one-fiftieth of an hour — about $1\frac{1}{2}$ minutes.

Werner Herzog is probably the only film director to have made a film with the entire cast, except one, under hypnosis.

There are more than 30,000 catalogued varieties of rose.

Errol Flynn and the Emperor Nero both competed in the Olympic Games — Flynn at boxing and Nero at chariot-racing.

Chelsea Pensioners wear scarlet frock-coats in the summer and navy tunics in the winter.

The varnish of a violin affects its tone.

According to Rolls Royce, their cars never break down. They simply 'fail to proceed.'

St Paul's Cathedral was the first British building to be fitted with a lightning conductor.

* *Never a Dull Moment* was, despite its title, rather a dull down-on-the-ranch comedy of 1950.

M·A·S·H

Aristotle thought that camel meat was the most delicate of all.

The Swedes are the world's greatest coffee drinkers. They average more than ten cups each a day.

In a survey of what children like and dislike eating, chips came out top and salad came out bottom.

To make authentic *chili con carne*, a piece of dark chocolate should be added to the meat mixture.

Ernest Hemingway wrote his books on a diet of peanut butter sandwiches.

Canadian scientists have come up with evidence that shows that women who eat salty foods and drink lots of tea and coffee tend to give birth to boys. Women who eat plenty of eggs and milk produce girls.

The most expensive cheese is La Barratte, which comes from France.

In Tibet, rancid yak butter is used in tea instead of milk.

Howard Hughes would eat only small peas. He had a special rake-like tool through which only the smallest peas would pass. He threw away those that didn't.

Vanilla is the best-selling ice-cream flavour.

The first frozen food available in Great Britain was asparagus.

A posset, often referred to by Shakespeare, was a concoction of hot, spice-flavoured milk curdled with wine or ale.

Cheshire is thought by experts to be the oldest variety of British cheese.

Roast armadillo is said to taste like pork.

Eskimos are partial to seal meat boiled in salt water.

The average Briton eats a large loaf of bread each week.

The Scots eat more cake and biscuits than people in any other part of Great Britain.

* *M*A*S*H*, which was made in 1970, was so successful as a film that it led to a TV series. For once, the TV series was as good as the film!

Law And Disorder

The game of bowls was once
banned in England. It was so
popular, it distracted men from
practising archery.

In 1694 Queen Mary died and barristers went into
black robes of mourning. They're still wearing them.

A French executioner was sacked after
pawning his guillotine.

The Scottish inventor of the first two-wheeled, self-
propelled bicycle was prosecuted for dangerous
driving.

When parking meters were first
introduced in the USA, furious drivers
beheaded them with axes.

The wearing of tartan was banned from 1746 to 1782.

In 1620, Oliver Cromwell was publicly
denounced for participating in the
'disreputable' game of cricket.

William the Conqueror decreed that after the tolling
of the eight o'clock bell everyone should put out their
lights and go to bed.

King Amunallah of Afghanistan stayed in London after the Great War and was so impressed by what he saw that when he got home he tried to pass a law requiring his male subjects to wear bowler hats.

The Queen's dogs do not require licences.

Hanging is still on the statute books for the crimes of treason and piracy with violence.

The Icelandic Parliament, known as the Althing, is the oldest surviving parliament in the world. It was founded in AD 930.

The first man to be convicted on fingerprint evidence was Harry Jackson in 1902.

A sixteenth-century English law allowed men to beat their wives — but only before 10 pm.

* There have been three films entitled *Law and Disorder*. The best of them was the one made in 1958 starring Michael Redgrave and Robert Morley in an Ealing-esque comedy.

London Town

Rudolf Hess was the last prisoner to be kept in the Tower of London.

Green Park was once a popular spot to fight a duel.

London's main Post Office sorting depots are linked by their own underground railway.

In 1381 the wife of Sir Robert Knollys built an illegal bridge over a road to connect her house and rose garden. She was fined — and the occasion is commemorated each year by the presentation of a rose to the Lord Mayor at the Guildhall.

Although the Great Fire destroyed much of the city, only six people were killed.

There are more than 400 blue plaques in London commemorating the places where famous people have lived and worked.

The Bank of England has its own artesian well.

Until 1764, London houses were not numbered.

In 1580, the building of new houses was banned because the city was getting too crowded.

There are a dozen secret rivers flowing beneath London. The Effra runs under the Oval cricket ground.

The highest concentration of rats in London is beneath the Houses of Parliament.

About 75,000 umbrellas are lost each year on London Transport.

Samuel Johnson's friend, James Boswell, found St James's Park the best spot for assignations with prostitutes.

Piccadilly gets its name from a men's collar. In 1630, a tailor who had made his fortune selling these 'picadillas' built a house called Picadilla Hall to the west of the City.

The nursery rhyme 'London Bridge is Falling Down' may date from 1014, when King Olaf of Norway hitched his Viking ships to an early bridge and pulled it down.

* *London Town* (1947) was supposed to be *the* new British musical. Alas, it was an expensive and totally disastrous flop, though it didn't manage to ruin the career of one of its young stars — Petula Clark.

Made For Each Other

Prostitutes in ancient Greece made use of sandals with the invitation 'Follow me' tooled in relief on the soles. As they walked along the dusty streets, they left a trail that clients could follow.

The Coventry Climax engine used in the Lotus Elite was developed from a fire pump.

Paper made from rags was first developed in the twelfth century, but scribes didn't like writing on its rough surface. It was ignored until the printing press came along, for which it proved perfect.

Nancy Reagan first met Ronald when she asked for his help in removing her name from a list of communist sympathizers.

Shredded wheat was originally invented for people with stomach disorders.

Accents were first introduced into written French during the reign of Louis XIII.

The first sign language for deaf mutes was invented by a Portuguese in 1749.

Battersea Park was once a swamp, but it was reclaimed by dumping soil excavated from the Royal Victoria Docks.

The Ecuadorian government wanted to erect a statue to their national poet, Jose Olmedo, but couldn't afford a new one. Fortunately, a statue of Lord Byron came on to the market and they snapped it up. Whether Byron and Olmedo looked like each other is not known.

Kleenex tissues were originally developed as gasmask filters during World War I.

The Chinese typewriter has 5,850 characters and even experts find it difficult to type faster than eleven words a minute.

The Coronation Chair in Westminster Abbey was originally made for Edward I.

* *Made For Each Other* was a 1938 tearjerker starring Carole Lombard, James Stewart and Charles Coburn. Carole Lombard and Clark Gable were one of Hollywood's most glamorous couples, yet at home they called each other Ma and Pa.

A Man To Remember

Scunthorpe was named after a squinting Danish pirate, though not many people remember him now.

Harvey Kennedy was the man who invented the shoelace and made a fortune from it.

The first recorded caesarean birth was carried out in 1500 by a man who was a pig gelder by profession.

The classic graffiti phrase *Kilroy was here* was originated by James Kilroy, who was employed in a World War II shipyard to inspect warships under construction. On everything he inspected he wrote *Kilroy was here* to prove he'd checked it.

The nineteenth-century bullfighter Lagartijo killed over 4,500 bulls during his career.

St Cuthbert was noted for his running and jumping abilities.

The British Museum was founded on the private collection of Sir Hans Sloane.

More books have been written about Jack the Ripper than about any other murderer.

The parking meter was invented in 1935 by Carl Magee.

The inch was defined by Henry III as the length covered by three barleycorns placed in a row.

Nicotine is named after the French ambassador to Portugal who in the 1500s brought tobacco to France.

The saxophone is named after its inventor, Antoine Sax.

Good King Wenceslas was a real king of Czechoslovakia.

You can recognize a messenger of the Bank of England by his pink coat and scarlet waistcoat.

* *A Man to Remember*, made in 1948, was one of those films it's best to forget. Even its stars, Edward Ellis and Anne Shirley, were immediately forgettable!

How To Be Very Very Popular

Don't be a man, be a mouse! Mickey Mouse was so popular that in 1933 he received more fan mail than any human performer.

To make their visitors feel at home, Eskimo men used to lend them their wives.

Henry VIII was popular with the ladies-in-waiting at his court after giving them an allowance of two loaves, a joint of beef and a gallon of ale each day for breakfast.

Male emus are popular with female emus because the males incubate the eggs.

Janis Joplin gave the makers of Southern Comfort so much free publicity that they gave her a fur coat.

Stamp collecting is the world's most popular collecting hobby.

According to surveys carried out in art galleries, Picasso is the most popular artist in the world.

Thomas Otway was killed by the kindness of an unknown benefactor who gave him a guinea when he was starving. Otway used the money to buy a roll and choked to death on it.

It has been estimated that during the first year of their marriage Aristotle Onassis spent more than $20 million on Jackie Kennedy.

Mao Tse-tung's Little Red Book became a best-seller at number two in the world, just behind the Bible — because Mao insisted that everyone in China should have a copy.

More books have been written about Shakespeare, Dante, Goethe and Cervantes than about any other writers.

In 1631, Charles I fined printers Barker and Lucas £1,000 for leaving a vital word out of their edition of the Bible. Verse 14 of Chapter 20 of Exodus reads: 'Thou shalt commit adultery.'

* *How to be Very Very Popular* was a wacky 1955 comedy about two belly-dancers on the run. It starred Betty Grable who, though she was billed as 'The Star with the Million Dollar Legs', actually had her pins insured for $1,250,000.

Handle With Care

As early as 246 BC, con men were at work 'ageing' manuscripts and selling them to book collectors as antiques.

Nelson's body was preserved in a barrel of rum for the journey back to England from the battle of Trafalgar.

A runcible spoon is not a spoon — it's a curved three-pronged fork.

When the first duck-billed platypus arrived at the British Museum, the curators thought it was a fake and tried to pull its beak off.

Cherry leaves are poisonous.

Copies of the Bible and of the Koran small enough to fit into a walnut shell have been written by hand.

Sidewinder snakes move in their peculiar fashion so as to avoid putting too much of their body area on the hot desert sand.

Carrots can kill. Just two mouthfuls of cowbane, a member of the carrot family, is enough.

The world's chickens lay around 400,000,000,000 eggs each year.

The cashew nut is a member of the poison ivy family.

Howard Hughes insisted on storing his urine in large glass bottles in a garage near his home. He employed an assistant to count and look after them.

Crocodiles kill about 2,000 people each year.

Before American football players venture on to the field, they don about 6 kg (13 lb) of protective clothing.

The largest crabs in the world, weighing more than 13 kg (28 lb) are found off the coast of Japan.

In the eighteenth century, many women went to the trouble of having their gums pierced so that they could use hooks to secure their false teeth.

* *Handle With Care*, was a 1958 melodrama. It starred an actor called Walter Abel who made his name with just one performance, which he used in every film he made! He specialized in playing a nervous, harassed character, usually the leading man's best friend or the heroine's father.

Gone With The Wind

The gold roof of Cracow cathedral was dissolved by acid rain.

The flying frog comes from Java and glides around supported by the webs of skin which grow between its feet.

In 1818, American celebrations of the Fourth of July were interrupted by a snowstorm.

The British Beaufort Scale for measuring wind force extends to 12, but the Americans, who suffer more severe weather, continue it to 17.

The last London smog occurred in 1962.

In Iowa in 1962, a cow flew nearly a kilometre (half a mile) after being sucked up in a tornado.

Scientists experimenting with carnivorous plants have discovered that although they love steak, cheese gives them terminal indigestion.

A fog belt 15 metres (50 ft) deep over an area of 270 square kilometres (104 square miles) contains no more moisture than a single bucket of water.

Crocodiles carry about 2.5 kg (5½ lb) of pebbles in their stomachs to counter indigestion.

Flies take off backwards.

The energy released in only ten minutes of a hurricane equals the output of the world's nuclear power stations.

Hailstones weighing 750 g (1½ lb) each fell over Coffeyville, Kansas in 1970.

At any one time there are 1,800 thunderstorms taking place in the world.

❝ Before starting work on Hurry Sundown, in which I played a man from the southern states, I happened to meet Vivien Leigh in a restaurant and asked her how she got her accent for Scarlett O'Hara." I used to say 'Four-door Ford' all day long," she answered. "Keep repeating it and everything you say will come out Southern." Try it — she's right. ❞

*   *Gone with the Wind* has probably been seen by more people than any other film in the world. Made in 1939, it starred Vivien Leigh and Clark Gable; she didn't like kissing him because she said that he had bad breath.

In Name Only

**The full name for Bangkok, capital
of Thailand, contains 169 letters.**

**The ballpoint pen was invented by the Biro
brothers.**

**In 1975 the most popular first names in
the US were Jennifer and Michael.**

America's first guide dog was called Buddy.

**Tangerines are so called because they
were first imported from Tangier in
Morocco.**

Mickey Mouse was originally called Mortimer.

Jim Callaghan's first name is Leonard.

**William Caxton, who first brought printing to
England, was assisted in his work by the
appropriately named Wynkyn de Worde.**

**Pop group Duran Duran took their
name from the villain in the film
Barbarella.**

Walt Disney's middle name was Elias.

The name 'Impressionists', used to
describe a nineteenth-century school of
painting, came from Monet's work
entitled *Impression, Sunrise*.

Mount Everest is known to Tibetans as Sacred
Mother of the Waters.

The Queen's first corgi was called
Susan.

The Latin name for the North American bison is
Bison bison.

The first recorded use of a double
Christian name was in 1608.

Margarine is named after the Greek for 'pearl'.

Ant-eaters are also known as
pangolins.

*   *In Name Only* was a rather heavy
matrimonial drama — not ideal for its
stars, Cary Grant and Charles Coburn.
When he died in 1961, Coburn was
cremated and had his ashes scattered in no
fewer than five places, in accordance with
his wishes.

Keep Fit

When he felt ill, Emperor Menelik II of Ethiopia used to eat a few pages from the Bible. Shortly before he died, he consumed the entire Book of Kings.

Jim Fixx, the guru of jogging, dropped dead while out on a run.

Kangaroo meat is cholesterol-free.

The three-toed sloth doesn't seem to believe in exercise. It moves so slowly that plants grow on its back.

Banging your head against a wall burns 150 calories an hour.

Leaf-cutting ants are so strong that they can carry a weight of vegetation equivalent to a child carrying a 10-ton truck.

The elephant seal is the most supple mammal.

Catherine the Great prescribed sex six times a day as a cure for insomnia.

Ostriches can swim. So can moles.

A caterpillar has more muscles than a man.

James Lind discovered in 1747 that lemon juice cured scurvy — nearly two hundred years before the discovery of vitamin C.

There are five different types of yoga.

Women suffer from chilblains more frequently than men.

The first antibiotics were developed in ancient Egypt, where people were treated with mouldy bread.

The avocado pear is the most fattening fruit.

Roman epileptics were prescribed a medicine made of fresh gladiator blood — so don't knock the NHS!

In the four years from 1966 to 1970, Howard Hughes, who was a hypochondriac, absorbed the equivalent of 3,000 codeine tablets.

* *Keep Fit* was a 1937 vehicle for George Formby — who was surely the world's only ukelele-playing film star!

You Never Can Tell

None of the widely-used household disinfectants can accurately claim to be 100 per cent effective.

Tobacco need not be harmful. It can be turned into a valuable source of protein.

Blancmange was originally a savoury dish.

A sea lemon is a variety of sea slug.

The nursery rhyme 'Ring a Ring o' Roses' refers to the marks caused by the plague.

Pygmy possums were thought to have been extinct for many years until one was discovered in Australia in 1966. Since then, more have been found.

Bears are right- and left-handed, just like people.

Research into weather proverbs has proved that 'Red sky at night, shepherd's delight' is true most of the time.

The heart does not lie on the left side of the body, as is commonly supposed. It is almost exactly in the middle.

The cigarette lighter was invented before the match.

Dinosaurs used to suffer from tooth decay.

Eau de Cologne was invented as protection against the plague.

Eskimos use refrigerators to prevent their food from freezing.

Scientists report that 15 per cent of people chew their toenails in secret.

In Georgian England, gentlemen used to eat animal testicles, believing they were aphrodisiacs. The most sought-after were lions' testicles.

* The story-line of *You Never Can Tell* (1951) took a bit of swallowing — it was about a murdered Alsatian dog that returned to earth as a private detective to track down its killer. Some people must have liked it, but you never can tell!

Thank Your Lucky Stars

French novelist Eugene Sue obviously considered himself lucky when his mistress died and willed him her skin to bind a book. He used it.

President Truman wasn't quite so lucky. His mother-in-law, who lived with him and his wife for 33 years, didn't like him, and never tired of telling him how much better other candidates would have been at the job.

John Jacob wasn't lucky either. When he reached the age of 120 his daughter sold him to a showman who exhibited him at fairs.

The Romans believed that it was bad luck to enter a house by the left foot, so they posted a servant at the door to make sure everyone entered properly — hence the term *footman*.

An Italian sculptor who had made a statue of the King of Poland trampling a Turkish soldier was less than pleased to discover that the Poles couldn't afford it. Luckily the British needed a statue to commemorate the restoration of the monarchy after Cromwell's Commonwealth and after a few necessary changes had been made, it was shipped to England. Many observers must wonder why Cromwell is portrayed wearing a turban.

Some Danes believe that each family has a special elf who lives in the house with them. When they move, their invisible friend goes with them. They leave the back of the furniture van open for a few moments when it's loaded so that they're sure he's climbed in safely.

In the fifteenth century Chinese scholars started work on an encyclopaedia containing 22,937 volumes. Two copies of this work were made, but every single volume has been lost.

Residents of Ireland and New Zealand count themselves lucky that their countries have no indigenous snakes.

In the US, anyone unlucky enough to be kidnapped has the assurance that any money paid out in ransom will be deducted from their income tax bill.

The doctor who delivered James II's son was knighted by the delighted king.

* *Thank Your Lucky Stars* was made in 1943 and succeeded in its intention of cheering up the war years. It featured more than a dozen stars, including Humphrey Bogart, Bette Davis and Errol Flynn — who must be the only Tasmanian to have become a major film star. Merle Oberon, who always said that she was from Tasmania, was in fact brought up in India.

The Way We Were

In Saxon times, Gatwick was a goat farm.

In the mid-nineteenth century, Turkish newspapers were strictly censored. When the king and queen were murdered, it was reported that they had died from indigestion.

In 1600 a pair of silk stockings cost £1.25.

The English habit of eating things on toast comes from the time when thick slices of bread were used instead of plates.

Dogs small enough to get through a gap 18 by 13cm (7 by 5 inches) were permitted to roam in William I's royal forests. Any larger dogs were killed because of the threat they posed to the deer.

Cricket, croquet, motorboating, rugby union and tennis have all been represented at the Olympics in the past.

The minute hand first appeared on watches in 1670.

At the court of King James I, young girls went bare-breasted as a sign of virginity.

The court of William Rufus, son of William the Conqueror, was famous for its women wrestlers.

While in Europe Neolithic man was beginning to go through the Bronze Age, Egyptians and Sumerians were building pyramids, establishing agricultural systems, playing the clarinet, making mirrors and writing poetry.

The world's first publishers may have been the Egyptian undertakers who included a copy of the *Book of the Dead* with each corpse they buried.

In America, tomato ketchup was patented as a medicine in 1830.

When the first public lavatories for women were opened in London in 1852, only twenty-four women used them in the first twelve months.

* *The Way We Were* (1973) is chiefly remembered for Marvin Hamlisch's Oscar-winning title song and for its stars, Barbra Streisand and Robert Redford. In 1968, Streisand tied with Katharine Hepburn for the Oscar for Best Actress, the first-ever tie for the title.

20,000 Leagues Under The Sea

Dolphins are only ever half asleep. Each side of their brain shuts down alternately.

Starfish can turn their stomachs inside out.

7,500,000 tonnes of water evaporate from the Dead Sea each day.

There are as many molecules in a spoonful of water as there are spoonfuls of water in the Atlantic Ocean.

The Sargasso Sea is not defined by a shoreline — it is completely surrounded by the Atlantic Ocean. And it's not covered in thick seaweed, as legend has it.

King James I was a passenger in the first submarine.

Kangaroos are excellent swimmers. One was caught swimming more than a mile off the shore of Australia.

The US Navy has trained dolphins and whales to retrieve missiles and debris from depths of nearly 600 metres (2,000 feet).

A blue whale, harpooned by a fishing boat, towed the boat at 11 km/h (7 mph) for several hours, even though its engines were in full reverse.

When an octopus becomes upset, it may eat itself.

Scientists have discovered vast underwater rivers which travel from the polar icecaps along the bottom of the ocean bed.

A giant squid with tentacles 36.5 metres (120 feet) long and a body more than 2 metres (6 ft 6 in) across has been swept ashore in the US.

‘ *James Mason is one of the quietest actors I've ever come across, but one of immense power. Kirk starred in* Champion, *the film that first inspired me to become an actor. I saw it every one of the six days it was running in the Elephant and Castle. I didn't think I could become a Kirk Douglas, but I thought I stood a chance as Arthur Kennedy who played his brother.* ’

* Kirk Douglas and James Mason were the stars of the ripping 1954 Jules Verne-inspired *Twenty Thousand Leagues Under the Sea*. The same year, Mason was invited to star with Alan Ladd in *Botany Bay*, but he declined on the grounds that he didn't want to have to stand in a trench for his scenes with Ladd — who was only 1.68 metres (5 ft 6 in) tall.

Doctor No

In 1635, the sale of tobacco was banned in France, though it could be obtained with a doctor's prescription.

A favourite medicine until the eighteenth century was powdered mummy — made from Egyptian mummies.

For many centuries, doctors examined their female patients in darkened rooms and underneath sheets, and if a man had to deliver a baby he did it without looking.

An American doctor has used hypnosis to enlarge his female patients' breasts. He says it works.

English folk-medicine recommends rubbing a tom-cat's tail in the eye to cure sties.

The suicide rate of female doctors is 60 per cent higher than the average female suicide rate.

Mediaeval man was fond of an operation called trepanning, which involved drilling a hole in the top of the head.

Doctors have recently begun to diagnose conditions such as Jogger's Nipple, Aerobics Ankle and Cyclist's Genitalia.

The bit of the nose that separates the nostrils is known as the Columella nasi.

Approximately 500 new human illnesses are discovered each year.

Viper flesh was recommended by doctors as an antidote to old age.

A Dublin doctor recommended filmgoers to wear dark glasses and to watch the screen for no longer than a minute at a time in case they were blinded.

The Incas were the world's first dentists.

❝ *When I first met Sean Connery many years ago it was at a party, and we got talking about how we had started in show business. He told me that he was the holder of a body-building title in Scotland at the time when Joshua Logan was casting* South Pacific. *He needed chorus boys who could sing "There's Nothing Like a Dame" and as the average British chorus boy wasn't exactly convincing, Logan ended up casting the show in body-building gyms. That's how Sean got into the business.* **❞**

* *Doctor No* was the first of the James Bond films. Produced in 1962, one of its best-remembered moments was when Ursula Andress walked from the sea in her bikini. The following year she participated in the first nude screen test for *Four For Texas*. She needn't have bothered; all the nude scenes were cut by the censor.

These Three

Sophia Loren, Chuck Berry and Al Capone were all prosecuted for tax evasion.

Elizabeth Taylor, T.S. Eliot and Henry James all renounced their American citizenship and became British subjects.

Nelson, Jack the Ripper and Judy Garland were all left-handed.

Sir Francis Drake, George Washington and Christopher Columbus were all slave-owners.

General Custer, Princess Grace of Monaco and Winston Churchill all slept with their dogs on their beds.

Walt Disney, Edward III and Mickey Rooney were all at one time bankrupt.

Gandhi, Napoleon and Sigmund Freud all suffered from constipation.

Mozart, General Tom Thumb and George Washington were all born in January.

The Salvation Army, the first Oxford and Cambridge boat race and the first London omnibuses all came into being in the same year — 1829.

Lawrence of Arabia, the Marquis de Sade and Dolly Parton all reached the same mature height of less than 1.67 metres (5 ft 6 in) tall.

Joan of Arc, Martin Bormann and Thomas à Becket were all put on trial after their death.

Ernest Hemingway, Bertrand Russell and Mark Twain all had premature obituaries published.

W. Somerset Maugham, Walt Disney and Ernest Hemingway all drove ambulances during World War I.

Oscar Wilde, Adolf Hitler and Miguel de Cervantes all wrote their major works in prison.

George Washington, James I and Henry Ford all grew or ordered marijuana to be grown — though at the time they thought of it as hemp.

*   *These Three* (1936) had a strong female cast of Merle Oberon, Miriam Hopkins and Bonita Granville. Oberon was most famous for her portrayal of Cathy in *Wuthering Heights*; her death scene in that film has gone down as one of the longest in history.

A House Is Not A Home

The *Grande Galerie* at the Louvre was used by King Henry IV for miniature fox hunts on wet days. Trees, rocks and grass were all brought in to make it more realistic.

Roman children used to play with dolls' houses.

Frank Lloyd Wright, the famous American architect, once planned a building a mile (1.6 km) high with 528 storeys and decks for 300 helicopters.

75 per cent of the contracts carried out by 75 per cent of British architects are for less than £75,000.

'Duchesses' and 'large ladies' are sizes of roofing tiles.

The Brazilian burrowing owl shares its home with armadillos, ant-eaters and even poisonous snakes.

Because of lack of building space in Tokyo, many flats and houses are tiny. A Japanese speciality is the 'capsule' hotel, where instead of rooms guests occupy tiny capsules only 2 m (6.6 ft) long and 1 m (3.3 ft) high, each equipped with sleeping mat and miniature TV.

Buckingham Palace is linked to Heathrow airport by a Tube line.

All household and electrical gadgets cause electrical and magnetic fields. Hair-driers have the greatest magnetic fields and electric blankets the greatest electrical fields.

Greenwich Palace was the first to have glass in its windows.

Washing-up is the most widely disliked household chore.

The corridors in royal homes are perfumed with smouldering lavender incense before guests arrive.

When Wembley Stadium was built in 1922, half-a-million rivets were used.

The floors of Henry VIII's palaces were strewn with rushes to disguise the dirt.

* *A House is Not a Home* (1964), was about a famous New York brothel. It starred Shelley Winters and Robert Taylor, who managed to break into films despite the fact that he failed an early screen test for being too skinny.

The Ruling Class

Edward III's queen pawned her crown in Germany and it had to be redeemed by the state for 30,000 packs of wool.

In China, the number of pockets on the outside of your clothing is an indication of status. Ordinary people have two; Party officials have four.

The only foreign monarch to appear on an English coin is Philip I of Spain who appeared with his wife, Mary I.

The Princess of Wales' middle name is Frances.

Queen Christina of Sweden kept a tiny cannon which she fired at fleas.

King John was the first British monarch to have a dressing-gown. He was also exceptionally clean, taking two baths a month.

When the Queen travels abroad, she makes sure that she takes supplies of Harrods sausages, fruit cake, mint sauce and Malvern water.

George II died after falling off the loo.

Peers of the realm who had been sentenced to hang had the right to die by a silken rope and not the common hemp variety.

Charles I *should* have been pleased to sign the death warrant of Captain Blood, the man who nearly robbed him of the Crown Jewels. Instead he commuted the death sentence and gave Blood a generous pension.

The last head of state to be excommunicated was Juan Peron of Argentina, who abolished church taxes, eliminated feast days and legalized brothels and divorce. Presumably he's still waiting for heaven.

‘ *Peter O'Toole became famous in the play* The Long and the Short and the Tall, *in which I understudied him as Private Bamforth. I took over the part when Peter left and was equally fortunate with it. That play helped us all tremendously.*’

*   *The Ruling Class* featured Peter O'Toole in a 1971 satire on the aristocracy. The following year he starred as Don Quixote in the ill-fated *Man of La Mancha*, a film so dreary and depressing that even Sophia Loren, who'd been voted Queen of the Sea in 1948, couldn't cheer it up.

Safety Last

To keep her secrets safe, the Queen uses black blotting paper.

If you want a safe dog, buy a golden retriever. Statistics show that they bite people less frquently than other breeds.

According to insurance brokers, astronauts have the most dangerous jobs in the world.

In the 1930 Mille Miglia motor race Tadzio Nuvolari drove in the dark without headlights so that the race leader wouldn't know he was behind him. This dangerous tactic allowed Nuvolari to overtake and win the race.

The 1933 Morris motor car carried miniature traffic lights with red, yellow and green indicators which the driver used to signal his intentions.

The first trains travelled at speeds up to 120 km/h (75 mph), yet they had no brakes.

The Motor Car Act of 1903 fixed the speed limit at 32 km/h (20 mph).

In case of nuclear attack, the Eastbourne area is likely to be one of the safest spots in Great Britain. Oregon is reckoned to be the safest part of the US.

The two great Mexican pyramids, the Pyramid of the Moon and the Pyramid of the Sun, were built with mortar made of ground corn.

The Chubb lock was invented in 1818.

The dangers of microwaves were discovered when radar technicians began to develop cataracts.

A pair of glasses fitted with rearview mirrors has been patented in the US.

Safest drivers on British roads are aged between 50 and 54.

Iceland was the first country in the world to establish insurance against fire and plague.

Duelling is legal in Uruguay so long as the participants are registered blood donors.

* Harold Lloyd, star of *Safety Last* (1923), was famous for his timid, bespectacled boyish character who managed to get into sticky situations. His daring and very dangerous stunts set the standard that the rest of the industry followed.

Once Upon a Time in America

As commander in chief of the American forces, George Washington refused a regular salary and worked for expenses only. He came out $400,000 better off than he otherwise would have done. When offered the US Presidency, he volunteered to work for expenses again — but this time Congress insisted he have a fixed salary.

Film star Pola Negri was the first woman in Hollywood to wear toe-nail polish.

The world's only operative water-powered commercial snuff mill can be found in Massachusetts.

Theodore Roosevelt was the first American President to make an official tour in a car.

Mount Katahdin in Maine is the first part of the US to receive the sun's rays each morning.

In the last 20 years, America has produced 120 mass 'serial' murderers. In the rest of the world there have been only 40.

In 1848, the population of San Francisco was 800. But when gold was discovered only 160 km (100 miles) away it dropped to just seven.

It takes 63,000 trees to produce sufficient paper for one Sunday edition of the *New York Times*.

There are more Italians living in New York than in Rome — and more Irish than in Dublin.

A survey discovered that the average American woman's vital statistics are 36-29-39.

There are more analysts and psychiatrists in the US than there are postmen.

❛ *At the end of one of the Oscar ceremonies, John Wayne began conducting all the presenters in a chorus of "You ought to be in pictures". Clint and I were very embarrassed about this and crept so far up stage that we fell off the back.* ❜

* Sergio Leone, director of *Once Upon a Time In America* (1984), is best known for inventing the spaghetti western. His *A Fistful of Dollars* shot Clint Eastwood to fame in 1964, and since then Eastwood has never looked back. At 1.93 metres tall (6ft 5ins) he's not only the tallest major film star currently working in Hollywood but also the most bankable.

The Naked Truth

We all shed our entire skin once every four weeks.

Human skin, when tanned and made into leather, resembles pigskin.

Human beings come equipped with their own snuffbox. The anatomical snuffbox is the name given to the hollow which appears when the thumb is raised towards the wrist.

An adult inhales about one pint of air with every normal breath.

Blue eyes get lighter with age.

The human body contains about 80,000 km (50,000 miles) of veins and capillaries.

On average humans have 200 hairs per square centimetre (0.15 square inch) of scalp.

Each day, an average pair of feet loses half a pint of water in sweat.

The jaw muscles can work for longer than any other muscle without tiring.

The sound you hear when you hold a seashell to your ear is your blood pumping.

If you are left-handed, the nails on your left hand will grow faster than those on your right, and *vice versa*.

The average human body contains sufficient sulphur to kill the fleas on a dog.

A human heart will beat more than 2,500,000,000 times in 70 years.

There are 4,000 wax glands in the ear.

Tears contain a soothing antiseptic substance.

On average, we lose between 30 and 60 hairs a day.

* *The Naked Truth* was a black comedy starring Peter Sellers, released in 1957. Sellers became most famous for the Pink Panther films in which he played the bungling Inspector Clouseau. *The Trail of the Pink Panther* (1982) is the first film to have been made after the death of its star; it was pieced together from left-over bits of previous Pink Panther films.

99 and 44/100 Per Cent Dead

Human beings have been around for only 0.0002 per cent of the earth's history.

20 per cent of all road accidents in Sweden involve a moose.

70 per cent of the world's grapefruit comes from Florida.

25 per cent of Americans and Europeans catch four or more colds each year.

About 12 per cent of an egg's weight consists of its shell.

Plants are 90 per cent water.

Since World War II, known cases of venereal disease among homosexual men have gone up by 200 per cent.

In 1968, one in every thirty-two postmen was bitten by a dog.

An atomic clock can be made accurate to one second in every 150,000 years.

In a sex study, 45 per cent of American men said that they prefer to make love with the lights on — which is unfortunate, because only 17 per cent of American women prefer it that way.

Twenty-six per cent of the British population would like to see immigrants from Australia and New Zealand banned.

Seventy-six per cent of American men would be willing to have sex with a total stranger for a million dollars.

More than 65 per cent of the tea drunk in Great Britain during the 1700s had been smuggled into the country to avoid import taxes.

According to researchers, eating is the favourite pastime of American adults. Watching televison and do-it-yourself come next. Sex is eighth on the list, after fishing.

Richard is not a great singer but one of my all-time favourite songs is his version of "Macarthur Park".

* The strangeness of *99 and 44/100 Per Cent Dead*'s title extended to its plot — which might or might not have been intended to be funny. Richard Harris was the star of this 1974 flop, though he probably wished he hadn't been.

The Marrying Kind

In one year, 1536, Henry VIII's first wife, Catherine of Aragon, died; his second, Anne Boleyn, was executed, and he married his third, Jane Seymour.

Elvis Presley proposed to Ginger Alden in his bathroom, while he sat on the loo. Unfortunately, he died in the very same bathroom before they could marry.

The sight of his wife's pubic hair on their wedding night so appalled English writer John Ruskin that he gave up sex.

The dance of the seven veils originates from the Middle Eastern custom of brides wearing seven successive robes during the wedding ceremony.

The Duke of Windsor was so in love with Mrs Simpson that he refused to allow her to handle used money. Every day he gave her a wad of freshly-printed notes.

Freud's wife was famed for the care she took of him. She even put the toothpaste on his toothbrush.

Every time Joan Crawford changed husbands, she changed the name of her estate and all the toilet seats in the house.

The first wedding anniversary is a paper one.

A Royal Commission of 1868 reported that in Scotland 90 per cent of women were pregnant on their wedding day.

An increasing number of people are *not* the marrying kind; 40 per cent of births to teenage mothers in 1983 were illegitimate.

Thirty-one per cent of British marriages involve a divorced partner.

Only 1 per cent of married British men do the washing and ironing.

George IV spent most of his wedding night in the fireplace, unwilling to share his new wife's bed.

W.H. Auden married the daughter of Thomas Mann to enable her to obtain a British passport. The first time they met was on their wedding day.

* *The Marrying Kind* (1952) starred Judy Holliday and Aldo Ray. Benjamin Franklin once advised men who were thinking of marriage to look for an older woman because 'They are so grateful.'

That's Entertainment

To conserve metal, the Oscars awarded during World War II by the American Academy of Motion Picture Arts and Sciences were made of wood.

The Indian film industry is the most prolific in the world.

Spain has a patron saint of the cinema.

Judy Garland's false eyelashes raised $125 at auction in 1979.

The Japanese were the first to offer soft-porn films for mass audiences.

There have been no fewer than 58 filmed versions of the Cinderella story, including cartoon, pornographic and parody treatments.

Howard Hughes's film *Hell's Angels* used so much film that if it had been shown unedited it would have run for 23 days.

Heaven's Gate, directed by Michael Cimino, holds the world record for the most money lost on a film — $34.5 million.

When Dr Joseph Goebbels decided to make a mammoth Nazi epic, *Kolberg*, in 1943, the war effort was diverted to an artistic one; 187,000 people were involved, including units of soldiers withdrawn from the front. It was seen by fewer people than had actually appeared in it.

For release in Germany, most of the Nazi scenes in *The Sound of Music* were cut.

Ernestine Russell made the wise decision to use her middle name, Jane, when she entered show business.

The Roxy in New York was the largest theatre auditorium built since the fall of Rome. It had its own hospital, radio station and orchestra of 110 musicians.

Mussolini was once involved with a film featuring nineteen *papier mâché* elephants.

* *That's Entertainment* was a collection of highlights from MGM musicals. It was introduced by Elizabeth Taylor, Fred Astaire and Frank Sinatra, among others. Some of its best moments involve clips from Frances Gumm's movies. Who was Frances Gumm? She became Judy Garland!

How The West Was Won

Wild west pioneers who suffered from vermin-infested buckskins used to dry-clean them on ant hills. The ants chased out the lice and fleas — then you just had to get rid of the ants in your pants.

In 1871, a buffalo herd 40 km (25 miles) wide and 80 km (50 miles) deep containing as many as six million animals was recorded.

The last man to speak the Mohican language died in 1933.

When scalping their victims, Red Indians made a cut right around the head just above the ears — and then pulled hard.

Buffalo Bill is the most filmed of all wild west characters. He even played himself five times.

When the US Secretary of State bought Alaska from the Russians for two cents an acre, his decision was regarded as total madness by most of the American people.

In 1924, 59 Westerns were made in the US. In 1984, only three were made.

Although Westerns usually show horses pulling wagon trains across the American heartland, oxen were far more efficient and were used more often.

Potato crisps were invented by Red Indians.

Barbed wire was developed in 1874 for fencing off ranches.

Lacrosse was invented by Red Indians and they played it with several hundred players on each side.

American Indian civilisation reached a peak in about 1300, when multi-storey houses and large villages were built. No one knows why, after that, the Indians went into decline.

Indian totem poles represent family trees in the same way that English heraldic crests do.

* *How the West Was Won* was an all-star buckskin spectacular including Debbie Reynolds, Henry Fonda, James Stewart and Gregory Peck. Debbie Reynolds was once Miss Great Britain.

You Can't Win 'Em All

Customs officials once seized what they thought was a pornographic film entitled *Games in Bed*, only to discover that it was all about ways of amusing sick children.

The fine for an overdue US library book returned in 1968 was more than $22,000. It had been borrowed in 1823.

Yo-yos were once banned in Damascus because it was believed that they were causing a drought.

Plans for the historic first broadcast of BBC-2 were disrupted by a power cut which left the studio in darkness.

Bette Davis turned down the role of Scarlett O'Hara in *Gone with the Wind* because she thought her co-star would be Errol Flynn, and she refused to work with him.

The first public lottery was introduced in Germany in 1494.

Thomas Hardy, Virginia Woolf and Henry James all failed to win the Nobel Prize for Literature, though they were nominated.

Leonardo da Vinci was convinced that there were canals leading directly from the lungs to the male sexual organs.

The parachute hat, which was rather like an open umbrella attached to a chinstrap, was intended to be worn by people working high above the ground. Patented in 1879, it has not yet caught on.

The ancient Romans were certain that parsley stopped them from getting drunk, so they ate lots of it...

Charles VIII of France died in 1498 when, trying to be polite as he escorted his queen into a tennis court, he didn't look where he was going and fractured his skull on a low beam.

Tony Curtis was responsible for me giving up smoking cigarettes fifteen years ago when he kept taking them out of my mouth and stamping on them. Then he later hit the headlines himself for a different sort of smoking! You really can't win 'em all.

* *You Can't Win 'Em All* must just about have summed up the reactions of Tony Curtis and Charles Bronson to the cool reception of their 1970 comedy. Working with Curtis must have been a change for Bronson; he's usually teamed with his wife, Jill Ireland, with whom he's appeared fourteen times.

When In Rome

Sausages were banned in Rome
during the reign of the Christian
emperor Constantine the Great
because of their association with
sinful pagan festivities. A thriving
black market was soon set up.

Brittanicus, son of the emperor Claudius, was killed
in a particularly cunning way. Knowing that his
personal taster would try all his food, his enemies
served a harmless but very hot drink which was
duly tasted and declared to be safe. Then water was
added to cool it — the poison was in the water.

The Vatican city has the lowest
birthrate in the world.

Roman soldiers on patrol in cold climates used to
sting themselves with nettles; it made them feel
warmer.

The Romans had a god for everything,
including one who was supposed to
protect their crops from mildew.

There were 144 public toilets in Rome in AD 315.

Ancient Romans used lead in their food
to make it more easy to digest. They
also took lead to cure stomach upsets.
It has been suggested by some
historians that lead was responsible for
the downfall of the Roman empire.

The emperor Elagabalus left no perversion or cruelty outside his experience. He met a fitting end when he was murdered in a toilet and his body was thrown down a sewer.

The Romans had a vast number of ways of executing people. One of them was to put the victim in a barrel lined with spikes and roll him down a hill.

It took time and trouble to train wild beasts to tear people to death, so measures were taken to ensure that the animals were not injured. Before being thrown to them at feeding time, the slaves had their teeth removed and their arms broken.

One notorious Roman epicure called Aesop had a pie baked containing nothing but birds that could imitate the human voice. His son inherited the vice and, so legend has it, would eat only dishes that contained a powdered jewel.

*   *When in Rome* (1952) was an over-the-top story about a gangster who disguises himself as a priest. Its stars survived the experience, but working on films about Rome can be dangerous. During the filming of *Quo Vadis* in 1925, a hungry lion escaped on to the set and ate an extra. Its keepers hesitated before shooting it — after all, extras were ten a penny but lions didn't come cheap...

Fame Is The Spur

In 1567, the man who was famous for the longest beard in the world tripped over it going down a flight of steps and was killed.

When Clark Gable removed his shirt in a film to reveal that he was wearing no vest, sales of vests dropped 40 per cent almost overnight.

Houdini can be said to have been killed because of his fame. He boasted that his stomach could withstand any blow — and when he was ready and had his muscles flexed it probably could. However, when a fan put him to the test by punching him without warning, the great escape artist collapsed in agony and died later of peritonitis, having suffered an internal rupture.

Sparkling champagne was invented by a blind Benedictine monk who is still famous — Dom Perignon.

Popeye the sailor was the first cartoon character to have a statue erected to him. It was held in place by a mixture of cement and spinach.

Aristotle Onassis once worked as a telephone operator.

After James Dean's death in a crash, teenagers paid to sit behind the wheel of the smashed car.

Alfred, Lord Tennyson, always complained of people staring at him in the street, but he persisted in wearing a large sombrero and a long black cape in case he wasn't recognized.

The pavement outside Grauman's Chinese Theatre contains the imprints not only of stars' hands and feet but also Jimmy Durante's nose-print, Trigger's hoof-prints, and Betty Grable's leg-prints.

Shirley Temple made much of her fortune by reproducing and selling the dresses she wore in her films.

I don't think Michael Redgrave ever got the full credit or fame he deserved from his films, because he got inside a part so completely that it totally enveloped him as an actor, hiding his true greatness.

* *Fame is the Spur* starred Michael Redgrave in a 1947 story of political ambition. At least when Redgrave broke into pictures he didn't face the opposition of his family — but when Leopold McLaglen tried to move from the British film industry to Hollywood, his big brother Victor, who had already made a name for himself out there, took out an injunction to prevent another McLaglen coming on the scene.

If...

If the great pyramid of Cheops were pulled down and the stone used to build a wall around France, the wall would be 3 metres (10 feet) high.

If all the roads in the US were joined together, they would make a road which would stretch around the world about 150 times.

If a human mother were to bear a baby proportionate to the size of a mother panda and her baby, the human child would weigh just 100 grams (3½ oz) — or 1/800th of its mother's weight.

If the world's largest country, the USSR, were the size of a football pitch, the Vatican City would be no larger than a quarter of a postage stamp.

If people in the Middle Ages suffered from nightmares, they scraped lichen from a crucifix and ate it.

If Western Europe continues to sink at its present rate, in 200,000 years' time the Eiffel Tower will be under water.

If you look carefully at the night sky, you may see the stars of the Andromeda galaxy. If so, you will be seeing them as they were long before humans appeared on the earth, because Andromeda is 2.2 million light years away.

If the earth were to become a black hole, the force of gravity would have to increase sufficiently to compress all the matter on the planet to the size of a matchbox.

If the earth were the size of a marble, the moon would be a ball-bearing just touching it and the nearest star would be 86,000 km (53,000 miles) away.

If you had spent £1,000 a day every day since the birth of Christ, you would still not have spent £1 billion (one million million) by now.

If you fold a US dollar note 40 times in the same place, it should not tear. The paper it is printed on is specially strengthened.

If you had been wounded at the Battle of Crécy in 1346 your wounds might have been treated with spiders' webs. Soldiers carried boxes containing webs for the purpose.

* When *If...*, Lindsay Anderson's 1967 attack on the public school system, was released, critics thought there was some obscure symbolism in the cuts from colour to black and white. There was, in fact, a more down-to-earth reason. The film was running out of money and black and white film was cheaper than colour.

Oh What A Lovely War

When Alaric, king of the Goths, besieged Rome in AD 408 his ransom demands included 3,000 lbs (1,400 kg) of pepper.

Balaclava helmets and cardigans were both invented during the Crimean war.

When the Egyptian king Menephta defeated the Libyans in 1300 BC, he took as a souvenir the 1,300 penises of his dead enemies.

Tolstoy's classic novel *War and Peace* was originally entitled *All's Well That Ends Well*.

Income tax was first introduced by Pitt the Younger as a temporary wartime measure.

Until 1942 Victoria Crosses were made from the metal of guns captured at Sebastopol in 1855.

Egyptians so revered cats that the Persians once used them to win a battle. The Persians threw cats over the walls of the Egyptian fort they were besieging — and the Egyptians surrendered rather than risk injury to the cats in battle.

Since Bolivia became an independent country in 1825, it has experienced more than 180 revolutions.

The last sea battle using oar-powered ships was at Lepanto in 1571.

Before Royal Marines go yomping, they stick plaster over their nipples to prevent them from being rubbed raw as they march long distances over tough terrain carrying heavy packs.

At the outbreak of World War I, there were only fifty men in the US Air Force.

Tanks got their name when they were first shipped to France. For security reasons, they were packaged in crates which were supposed to contain water tanks — and the name stuck.

The last Roman soldier left Britain in AD407.

* *Oh What A Lovely War* had been a phenomenal success for Joan Littlewood's stage company and, adapted by Len Deighton and starring Olivier, Gielgud, Richardson and two Redgraves, Vanessa and Michael, the screen version should have been a triumph. Sadly, what worked on stage did not work on film and *Oh What A Lovely War* went down as one of the major disappointments of 1969.

The Man With Two Faces

A nineteenth-century Bishop of Raphoe spent his out-of-church hours as a highwayman on Hounslow Heath. He was shot there in 1850 by one of his victims.

French novelist Emile Zola had two families by his wife and mistress and lived with them both.

Because audiences saw only one side of him during performance, Chopin would sometimes shave only one half of his face.

Florence Nightingale, famous for her nursing work in the Crimea, was a hypochondriac. When she returned to England in 1856, she told everyone she had terminal heart disease and retired to bed — where she stayed for the next 54 years.

Douglas Fairbanks was so loved by his fans that when he wed Mary Pickford his married status was kept a secret.

Casanova, famed for his sexual exploits, spent the last thirteen years of his life working as a librarian.

Marie Stopes, the sex and birth-control campaigner, first learned about sex at the age of twenty-nine. Hardly the libertine opponents made her out to be!

Abraham Lincoln believed all his life that he was illegitimate and stood up publicly for bastards. It was only after his death that he was discovered to be legitimate.

The first man with two faces was probably the victim of an early plastic surgeon. In India, adulterers who'd had their noses chopped off were having skin grafts more than a thousand years ago.

After banning Charlie Chaplin's anti-Nazi satire *The Great Dictator*, Hitler couldn't resist obtaining an illegal copy — and watching it twice.

Rembrandt had more than two faces; he painted his self-portrait more than sixty times.

❝ *Eddie Robinson and I became close friends through a mutual interest in paintings. He died shortly before the Academy Awards at which I had been nominated for* Sleuth, *and a lifelong friend of his told me that Eddie's parting words to him had been, "Don't forget to vote for Michael." There was a friend for more than life.* ❞

* *The Man with Two Faces*, a revenge drama starring Edward G. Robinson, was released in 1934. Edward G. Robinson's name was originally Emanuel Goldenberg. He became Robinson after the name of a butler in a play he had seen, and Edward because it was the name of the king of England. The G was inserted in the middle at his insistence, to remind him of his Jewish origins.

Around the World in Eighty Days

About 450 million years ago, the South Pole was situated where the Sahara Desert is now.

Spinach originated in Persia.

The four shortest place-names in the world are A (Norway), U (the Caroline Islands), O (Japan) and Y (France).

The painted lady butterfly migrates more than 4,000 km (2,500 miles) from Africa and Asia to Europe.

On one of the Canary Islands, the mountain-tops are so close to each other that messages are sent by whistling in code between them.

The Australian city of Adelaide is named after King William IV's wife.

The whole of the American continent could be fitted into Asia with room to spare.

McBurney's Point isn't a geographical feature. It's a painful spot in the abdomen, caused by an attack of appendicitis.

In 1925, the Niagara Falls completely froze over.

Of the forty-eight known species of Bird of Paradise, thirty-eight are found in Papua New Guinea.

The game of chess originated in India.

Robert Louis Stevenson is buried in Western Samoa.

A nineteenth-century eccentric called John Allington taught his estate workers geography by building a scaled-down map of the world in a lake and taking them on rowing-boat tours of it.

Greece is the world's chief exporter of natural sponges.

More books are sold per head of population in Iceland than anywhere else in the world.

* *Around the World in Eighty Days*, made in 1956, featured no fewer than forty-four stars including David Niven, Noel Coward, John Gielgud, Buster Keaton, Marlene Dietrich and Frank Sinatra. In 1937, Dietrich had earned $450,000 for a single film, *Knight Without Armour*.

The Music Lovers

French composer Lully died after piercing his foot with the cane he used for conducting the orchestra and contracting blood poisoning.

A Japanese architect was hanged in 1974 for murdering a mother and two daughters because they would not stop playing the piano in a nearby flat.

Opera star Enrico Caruso was once arrested for pinching a lady's bottom in the Monkey House of New York City Zoo.

The composer Schoenberg was born on 13 September 1874 and was convinced that he would die on the thirteenth. He also believed that as the numbers seven and six make thirteen, he would die at the age of seventy-six. He died thirteen minutes before midnight on Friday 13 July 1951, aged 76.

Dame Nellie Melba, the Australian opera star, not only gave the world the peach Melba but also Melba toast.

Rossini was too nervous to travel by rail.

The composer Elgar used to go out driving with his three dogs in the back seat of his open car — all of them wearing goggles.

The Queen is entertained by bagpipe music at
breakfast each morning when a piper marches
outside the dining-room window for fifteen minutes.

The opera *Aida* was specially
commissioned to celebrate the opening
of the Suez Canal.

Handel's *Messiah* was first publicly performed in
Dublin.

Ravel composed only nineteen hours of
music over forty-two years.

La Monte Young's Piano Piece for David Tudor No.1
requires the pianist to feed the piano with hay and
water.

*‘ I don't know about his taste in music, but Richard
Chamberlain is a great Anglophile and loves working in
Britain. After Doctor Kildare he spent a lot of time working in
British regional theatres, and I've always felt deserved greater
recognition for his qualities as an actor.’*

* *The Music Lovers*, Ken Russell's film about
homosexual composer Tchaikovsky and his
marriage to a nymphomaniac, caused quite
a stir in 1970. Richard Chamberlain and
Glenda Jackson are remembered for it —
but who remembers that it was written by
Melvyn Bragg?

Close Encounters Of The Third Kind

When Marie Antoinette's horoscope was cast shortly after her birth, it predicted such disaster that the birth celebrations were cancelled.

Every time it is hit by a sizeable object, the moon makes a strange, and so far unexplained, ringing noise.

At least three women in Australia, England and the USA claim to have been raped by creatures from outer space.

Ball lightning has been seen to travel through aircraft, touching and harming nothing as it moves.

Much of the moon's surface is covered in a glass-like substance, the result of scorching by immense heat.

In 1908, a huge explosion ten times more powerful than the Hiroshima bomb was recorded in Siberia. Scientists examining the site could find no evidence of a meteorite or comet or any other explanation, and the case remains a mystery.

The first reward for communicating with an extra-terrestrial being was offered in 1900. However, Martians were not counted for the prize because they were thought to be too easy to contact.

Charles De Gaulle was a firm believer in astrology, having being told at an early age that his horoscope indicated he would be leader of France.

In 1951, a psychic horse called Lady Wonder directed police to the site of a missing child's body by tapping out her message on a giant typewriter with her nose.

Astronauts have to use special shavers that suck up the whiskers as they are cut.

❛ *Steven Spielberg has had a few close encounters in a restaurant I have a part share in London, where he likes eating when he is in town. "Can you tell the people in your restaurant who I am?" he asked me once, "because whenever I want to make a reservation I have to tell them I'm Harrison Ford!"* ❜

*   *Close Encounters of the Third Kind* was such a success when it was first launched in 1977 that director Steven Spielberg was able to afford to give it a new and improved ending and release it for a second time in 1980. The indoor set used for the film was the largest ever built.

Cat People

The most popular names for American cats in 1981 were Tiger and Samantha.

An Australian man who hated cats coming into his garden set a trap for them — a sardine tin wired to the electricity mains. His ploy backfired when he was electrocuted by his device.

Marie Curie's pet cat, Tabitha, was poisoned by acid when she crept into a cupboard in which an experiment was housed.

At Romford Greyhound Stadium in 1937, an attempt was made to stage a cheetah race. Alas, the cheetahs thought racing after a hare was beneath their dignity and punters lost their money.

A society to improve the moral and mental faculties of the domestic cat was founded in Belgium in 1877.

American cat-lover Governor Pinchot sentenced the dog that killed his cat to life imprisonment. The dog served six years.

Winston Churchill, Raymond Chandler and Samuel Johnson were all cat-lovers.

There was no such thing as a stray cat in ancient Egypt. All cats were fed and cared for.

The oldest cat ever recorded lived to the age of thirty-six.

President Eisenhower hated cats so much that he ordered any trespassing on his property to be shot.

When the restoration was under way of St Michael's Paternoster, a church built by Dick Whittington, workmen found a mummified cat.

In 1890, 180,000 mummified Egyptian cats were sold to a company to be made into fertilizer.

A Siamese cat survived a thirty-two day trip in the hold of an aeroplane that had taken it literally around the world.

The poet Shelley hated cats. He once tied one to the string of a kite he was flying in a thunderstorm to see if it would be electrocuted.

* The first version of *Cat People*, made in 1942, revolutionized horror movies by relying on suspense to terrorize the audience; it was the first monster film in which the monster wasn't actually seen.

Blockheads

In 1800, Claude St James published *How to Win at Poker*. A group of businessmen decided to invest in his system and raised half a million pounds for him to play with. He lost it all.

The builders of the Leaning Tower of Pisa used only 3-metre (10-foot) foundations.

Requested by Queen Victoria, who had enjoyed *Alice in Wonderland*, to send her another of his books, Lewis Carroll, who was a brilliant mathematician, sent her a book on algebra.

A Nigerian man agreed to help his local witch-doctor test a bullet-proof charm which the medicine man had invented. Unfortunately it didn't work, as they discovered when the volunteer was shot dead.

In the early 1970s, a new brand of soap powder was launched in Saudi Arabia with an advert showing a pile of dirty clothing on the left of the picture, a tub of soap-suds in the centre, and a stack of gleaming laundry on the right. The product did not do well; Arabs read from right to left.

The area known as Yucatan is so-called because when explorers first landed there and asked what it was called they received the reply *'Yukatan'* — 'I don't understand you.'

At the first modern Olympics held in Greece in 1896, a runner in the marathon was disqualified after using a horse and carriage to take a short cut.

Howard Hughes's assistants once left the air-conditioning on in an empty house for eight years because Hughes didn't tell them to turn it off.

In 1894, the trustees of the National Gallery turned down the chance to acquire a great Titian painting because it showed too much flesh.

President Reagan made an unfortunate slip of the tongue when, speaking about third-world countries, he said, 'The US has much to offer the third world war.'

6 I never met either Laurel or Hardy but for their honeymoon my parents went to the old South London Theatre in the Elephant and Castle and saw Stan Laurel on stage with Charlie Chaplin — that was after a wedding meal of jellied eels and before my father went to work the next morning.9

* *Blockheads*, made in 1938, is considered to be the last really great Laurel and Hardy film. Stan Laurel, by the way, was born at Ulverston in Cumbria.

Never On Sunday

Elizabeth I was not a stickler for observing the Sabbath. She danced on Sundays — but she didn't kick her legs as high as she did on other days.

Belgium has never exercised censorship over adult films, the only country not to do so.

Because of shortages of cloth during the war, male swimmers in some parts of the country were permitted to wear brief trunks at municipal swimming pools. But as soon as the shortages were over they were required to appear in more substantial garments.

Feet were so offensive to prudish Victorian Americans that the word *feet* was banned from conversation.

When Elvis Presley first appeared on television in 1956, he was shown only from the waist up so that his wiggling hips wouldn't offend viewers.

Mickey Mouse has been banned in Germany, Italy, Yugoslavia and Russia.

Until recently, an American organization fought to cover the sexual organs of animals, designing all kinds of elaborate nappies and overalls for them.

In the state of Minnesota, it is against the law to hang male and female underwear together on the same washing-line.

Charlie Chaplin's film *Limelight* was banned in the US for twenty years because of Chaplin's political stance. When it was eventually shown in 1972, it won an Oscar.

The makers of a 1952 art documentary were forced to cut a shot of a Botticelli nude because it was deemed offensive by the censor.

Nineteenth-century Valentine card makers dressed Cupid, traditionally naked, in a skirt.

The word 'cock' reduced modest Victorian Americans to blushing embarrassment, so the word 'rooster' was invented.

* Melina Mercouri was the star of the 1959 Greek movie *Never On Sunday*. These days she's the Greek Minister for Culture and most widely known for her battle to have the Elgin Marbles returned to Greece.

A Family Affair

The initials LBJ were common to President Lyndon B Johnson's entire immediate family.

In 1944, a French resistance fighter shot and killed two Nazi officers. It wasn't until the war was over and he was reunited with his family that he learned that one of the officers had been his mother's lover and was in fact his father. And the second officer was his father's brother — his uncle.

King Mongut of Siam had 9,000 wives and concubines.

The panda is a member of the raccoon family.

The Queen and Prince Philip are third cousins through their descent from Queen Victoria.

The Redgrave family have been in the acting business for four generations.

Family allowances were first introduced in 1945.

Thanks to artificial insemination, an American bull produced 15,000 offspring in less than $3\frac{1}{2}$ years.

One of the governesses to the Mitford family took the girls on shop-lifting sprees.

The Emperor penguin incubates its eggs on its warm toes, shuffling around with them for 64 days and nights on ice that can be as cold as -60°C.

Casanova nearly married his own daughter. Fortunately, the girl's mother appeared just in time for him to recognize her as a former lover and the marriage was called off.

The rabbit population of Australia is derived from just three pairs released in the nineteenth century. In less than ten years there were millions of them.

Pope Sergius III made arrangements for his bastard son to become pope after his death.

Garlic is a member of the lily family of plants.

The three golden balls used to indicate a pawnbroker's shop were originally part of the coat of arms of the Medici family of Italy.

* *A Family Affair* (1937), was the second film in a highly successful series about the Hardy family. It starred Mickey Rooney and Lionel Barrymore. Rooney would probably get along well with Ava Gardner; after all, they've both been married eight times.

Fear is the Key

Hans Christian Andersen was so frightened of dying in a fire that he always carried a rope to escape.

A survey undertaken in the US showed that only 19 per cent of those interviewed feared death more than anything else.

James I was so frightened of being assassinated that he wore a thickly-padded duvet-style coat for protection.

Many bright red berries are poisonous; for a long time tomatoes were thought to be killers.

After the Battle of Waterloo, people were fearful to wear or grow violets because they had been the favourite flower of Napoleon.

The Colt gun, known as an equalizer, was justly feared because it made a weak man equal to any other.

George Bernard Shaw lost his virginity at the age of twenty-nine and found the experience so shocking that he was celibate for the next fifteen years.

The strain of being Prime Minister was too much for the Earl of Rosebery. He resigned because the worry gave him insomnia.

A fifteenth-century criminal was so terrified by his death sentence that he agreed to be one of the first medical guinea pigs. He underwent an agonizing and dangerous operation, was sewn up — and survived to receive a pardon.

One of the most common of all fears is that of public speaking.

Mary Mallon spent the last twenty-three years of her life in prison because, through no fault of her own, she was a typhoid carrier.

Pognophobia is the fear of beards.

Japanese chefs have to train for three years before they are allowed to serve the puffer fish, a delicacy only for the brave. The fish contains one of the most dangerous poisons in the world and is lethal if not properly cooked and prepared.

* *Fear is the Key* was a 1972 British thriller based on an Alistair Maclean novel. It feature Ben Kingsley, who was later to achieve fame in *Gandhi*.

Reds

Differential gearing had been invented in China before the birth of Christ.

The USSR was the first country to legalize abortion.

In 1978, all the tea in China came to more than 350,000 metric tonnes.

The USSR has the largest number of public libraries and books in the world.

Kim Philby, highly successful Russian agent, was singled out by Churchill and Roosevelt as a likely candidate for Head of British Intelligence.

The speedometer was invented in China in AD 1027. The Chinese were also using cable suspension bridges in 100 BC.

One person in every four is Chinese.

Both China and Wales have the dragon as their national symbol.

The Chinese invented playing cards in AD 1120.

Twenty million people died of starvation and influenza in the USSR in the decade 1914-24.

Not only are Chinese books written back to front; the footnotes used to appear at the top of the page.

The three most common surnames in China are Chang, Wang and Li.

Robin Hood was banned in Indiana in the 1950 on the grounds that robbing from the rich to give to the poor was communism.

The USSR is the fourth-largest wine-producing country in the world.

The works of Dickens and Shakespeare were banned during the Chinese cultural revolution, but are now back on library shelves.

*   The heads of Paramount must have taken some persuading before they gave Warren Beatty $45 million to make *REDS* (1981), a film about the life of communist John Reed, a man so dear to Moscow's heart that he's actually buried in the Kremlin. They must have regretted it too, because though Beatty's film was an artistic success it has earned back less than half what was spent on it. John Reed would have approved!

Work Is A Four-Letter Word

An eighteenth-century chief cashier of the Bank of England was so conscientious that he spent twenty-five years in the bank, sleeping there every night.

In Paris, a select band of people made a living by attending dinner parties to boost the numbers from thirteen to fourteen. They were known as '*quatorzes*'.

After the Coal Mines Act of 1911, pit ponies' hours of work were limited to forty-eight per week with two weeks' annual holiday.

According to government statistics, in 1974 it took one hour and one minute for the average male worker to earn one pound of rump steak. In 1983 it took him only fifty-two minutes.

The fifth Duke of Portland's workers received a donkey and an umbrella as part of their wages.

The first newspaper crossword puzzle appeared in the *New York World* in 1913.

British and American architects have designed buildings for sites that they have never seen in Mecca and Medina, where non-Muslims are barred.

The word 'robot' is from the Slav word meaning 'work'.

In India, Sri Lanka and Costa Rica women grow most of the food, though most of the land is owned by men.

It was not unknown for guards on the Great Wall of China to be born there and live there until they died.

The first general strike occurred in Hamburg in 1791.

The Domesday Book records that there were more than 28,000 slaves in eleventh-century Britain.

In the eighteenth century, members of the Stock Exchange had access to their own private brothel.

Anne Boleyn had the unfortunate habit of vomiting during meals, so one of her ladies-in-waiting had to hold up a sheet to shield her from other diners at appropriate moments.

* Judging by the reaction of audiences to *Work Is a Four-Letter Word*, Sir Peter Hall, who directed it in 1968, is better off running the National Theatre.

Animal Crackers

The Incas are the first recorded people to have kept guinea pigs as pets.

A sledge pulled by ten dogs can travel about 19 km/h (12 mph).

The flying snake of south-east Asia glides from tree to tree.

The cat, the camel and the giraffe all walk the same way, moving front and back legs on one side together.

Frogs respond more to blue light than to any other colour.

Both Mary Queen of Scots and Charles I were accompanied to their executions by their dogs.

300,000 Israeli cows have been issued with identity cards.

Queen Victoria won six prizes at Crufts in 1891 for her Pomeranian dogs.

Coffee, tobacco, sailcloth, sticky tape, engine oil and the American flag have all been found in polar bears' stomachs.

Snakes may have as many as 300 pairs of ribs.

The Queen has her own stable of 250 racing pigeons in King's Lynn. Each pigeon wears a ring with the initials ER.

The chameleon's eyes work independently so that it can look in two directions at once.

Dolphins have been used to guide stranded whales back to sea.

Alexander the Great named an Indian town Bucephala after his horse, Bucephalus, which used to kneel so that he could mount in full armour.

❝ The only Marx brother I ever met was Groucho and he was mad about my wife, Shakira. Every time we met at a party he used to say, "Michael, I want a drink — and the bar's in the other room." Then the minute I was out of the way, he would grab hold of Shakira, bend her over backwards and kiss her on the mouth! He must have been about eighty at the time but there was still plenty of animal and a lot of cracker.❞

* *Animal Crackers*, made in 1930, was a Marx Brothers picture. Harpo Marx, who adored children, once tried to adopt Shirley Temple. Sadly, the child-star's parents weren't keen on the idea.

Private Lives

Benjamin Franklin was a member of the Hellfire Club, which organised elaborate orgies and satanic rites.

The Marquis de Sade's mother was a nun.

President Lincoln had a secretary called Kennedy. President Kennedy had a secretary called Lincoln.

Jayne Mansfield's favourite colour was pink.

Mao Tse-tung started out as a librarian.

Charles V, once Holy Roman Emperor but forced into abdication, spent the last years of his life trying to make twelve clocks run in unison.

Actor and singer Kris Kristofferson started out as an American football star and was also a student at Oxford.

Diarist Samuel Pepys liked playing the recorder.

Prime Minister William Gladstone used to fill his stone hot-water bottle with tea. He seldom slept more than four hours, so when he woke up it was still warm enough to drink.

Angus Ogilvy was once a waiter at the Savoy, and Lord Snowdon was a waiter at a Brighton restaurant.

President Brezhnev was crazy about cars. Richard Nixon, knowing this, made him a gift of three.

Bob Hope started his career as a boxer.

In 1960, one London strip club included among its members ten MPs, sixty knights and thirty-five peers.

The Duke of Edinburgh was born on a dining-room table. Winston Churchill was born in a ladies' cloakroom.

Peter Ustinov's grandmother was half-Ethiopian.

George V was a renowned stamp collector.

* *Private Lives* suffered the fate of many a great stage play when it was made into a film in 1932; it had only a cool response. Its star, Norma Shearer, went on to appear in the 1939 film *The Women* which boasted 135 female speaking roles.

Mad About Men

The ancient Egyptians were mad about having male rulers, so when Queen Hatshepsut acceded to the throne she was officially portrayed with a beard and no breasts.

There are about two million exclusively homosexual men in Britain today.

Far from being a prude and a kill-joy, Queen Victoria had an active sex life with Albert and was most disconcerted when it was suggested that, to avoid further pregnancies, she should give it up.

Queen Zingua of Angola kept a well-stocked harem of men and often had them executed after a night of love.

Before Catherine the Great took on a new lover, he was inspected by her doctor and tried out by one of her ladies-in-waiting, who would report on his performance.

The male prostitutes of ancient Rome scratched their heads with their middle finger to indicate their business.

As early as the 1580s, doctors were discussing the possibility of breast augmentation and reduction for women.

In Italy, police who rounded up a ring of prostitutes were amazed to discover that they were all grandmothers.

Edith Piaf found it difficult to resist a man with blue eyes.

Anyone who is mad about men may find it useful to know that male sex hormones are at their peak in the autumn and winter.

In Hawaii, the age of consent for homosexuals is fourteen.

Film star Clara Bow was reputed to have taken on the entire University of Southern California football team in bed.

Archaeologists have discovered that Inca girls plucked their eyebrows, dyed their hair, powdered their faces — and carried their beauty kits with them in special handbags.

* Although *Mad About Men* sounds promisingly racy, it is a rather sedate English comedy, released in 1954 and starring Donald Sinden, Dora Bryan and Irene Handl.

It's Not Cricket

As Captain Valentine Todd made his approach to bowl in a cricket match being played at the siege of Ladysmith, he was killed by a passing shell. He fell holding the ball, which could not be prised from his fingers, and a quick umpiring decision was required before the game could be resumed. Both ball *and* bowler were declared dead.

A survey of more than 3,000 athletes revealed that 22 per cent of them wear glasses.

Table tennis was originally played with a cork ball.

Cricket was outlawed in 1477 by Edward IV.

Referees in the Super Bowl series of American football matches can expect to earn about £2,500 per match.

The first floodlit football league game was played in 1956.

There are seven players in a water polo team.

In 1771, the rules of cricket were changed to outlaw bats wider than 4½ in (114 mm) after one player walked on to the field with a bat wider than the wicket.

In the days when golf balls were filled with feathers, it took a top-hat full of feathers to stuff a single ball.

Billiards was first played in Italy in 1550.

The longest boxing match on record was over 110 rounds and took seven hours and nineteen minutes to complete. Even then, there was no winner, because both contestants were ruled unfit to continue.

Arsenal football club started out as Dial Square FC in 1884.

An event called *plunging* was included in the 1904 Olympics. Competitors had to dive in from the side of the swimming-pool and float as far as possible in one minute.

Ski slopes are graded by colour according to their difficulty.

* As far as most critics were concerned, the cast of *It's Not Cricket*, (GB 1948), weren't given a sporting chance to show what they could do.

Nothing Sacred

Pope Pius II once scolded one of his cardinals for wearing his robes to an orgy.

In 1869, the governor of Burgos in Spain was stabbed to death in a cathedral, during Mass, by a group of priests.

The Russian for God is *Bog*.

William Buckland, Dean of Westminster, stole the heel of poet Ben Jonson when Jonson's grave was disturbed in 1849. It turned up again in a junk shop in 1938.

Charles Darwin, whose book *On the Origin of Species* rocked the Church, once trained for Holy Orders.

Ancient Indian temple priestesses used to have sex with male worshippers for money for the temple coffers.

The earliest form of lawn tennis was played by French monks.

The head of the Roman Catholic church in the Philippines is Cardinal Sin.

The first knitting machine was invented in 1589 by a clergyman.

The vicar of Warleggan in Cornwall was so disliked by his parishioners that they stopped going to church. Undeterred, the vicar filled the pews with cardboard effigies and preached to them each Sunday.

In 1980, a North Carolina library forbade children to read the Bible without parental permission.

In Wales in the sixteenth century, forty-three clergymen were listed as having concubines.

The wedding of Henry I to his queen, Adelaide, was held up by a bitter row when the king insisted on wearing his crown throughout the ceremony and the priest objected.

A Swedish pastor was electrocuted as he stood in a pool of water for a baptism ceremony when one of his assistants handed him a live microphone.

* *Nothing Sacred* was one of the best American films of 1937. A zany comedy, it starred Carole Lombard who, having started life as plain Jane Peters, renamed herself after a chemist's shop called the Carroll Lombardi Pharmacy.

Nasty Habits

The common housefly has such filthy habits that it transmits as many as thirty different diseases to man.

In China, children of three and four years old regularly enjoy a cigarette.

Vultures have no feathers on their heads because of their habit of thrusting them into dead carcasses.

When the poet Rossetti's wife died, he buried her with a book in which he had written all his poems. Seven years later, he changed his mind and decided that he'd like them back. The grave was opened and the poems removed and disinfected. They were later published, to general acclaim.

Scientists studying cannibalism have shown that a man weighing around 68 kg (150 lb) would make a meal for seventy-five people.

When the King of Siam wanted to dispose of one of his relatives, he remembered the traditional belief that royal blood should never be spilt on the ground — so had the unfortunate victim pounded to death in a large pestle and mortar. The blood was contained in the vessel and not a drop touched the ground.

In 1624, Pope Urban III threatened to execute snuff users because of their dirty habit.

The Incas of Peru used to treat headaches by bleeding themselves between the eyebrows.

Our word 'loo' is taken from the French phrase '*Gardez l'eau*' which was shouted as householders emptied their chamberpots into the street.

Viscount Colville had a glass eye. He was so worried that he would lose it that he kept a spare one in a special gold globe dangling from his watch chain.

The butcher bird hangs its left-over meat on the thorns of a bush until it is ready to eat it.

The Albanians once issued a stamp to commemorate Ahmed Zogu I, whose distinction was his powers at smoking. He puffed his way through 240 cigarettes daily.

❛*An incident at the end of filming* The Romantic Englishwoman *confirmed for me that Glenda Jackson is one of the least actressy of actresses. I was flying to the French Riviera for the weekend and asked her what she was doing. "Well, on Saturday morning I'll be in Sainsbury's," she said.*❜

* *Nasty Habits* was a 1976 satire of the Watergate scandals, set in a convent. It starred Glenda Jackson, who five years earlier had starred in *Sunday, Bloody Sunday*, a benchmark in the film industry because of its passionate homosexual kiss between Peter Finch and Murray Head. Afterwards the film's director, John Schlesinger, noted that the kiss had shocked the public less than it had the film's technicians.

Professor Beware

Pythagoras firmly believed that some human souls were transformed into beans after death.

Sir William Dewer, inventor of the vacuum flask, used one of them to keep milk warm for his baby son. However, his mother-in-law had no faith in the new contraption and knitted a special cosy to fit over it and retain the heat.

Isaac Newton solved problems in his sleep.

In the nineteenth century, Lord Kelvin proved beyond all doubt that flight in a heavier-than-air machine was impossible.

Seventeenth-century scientist Francis Bacon believed that warm water freezes more quickly than cold water.

Attempting to humiliate Fidel Castro of Cuba by making his beard fall out, CIA scientists developed a powder that, if applied to his shoes, should have had the desired result.

Citric acid is not obtained from lemons — it is produced from mould.

Sir Humphrey Davy, Marie Curie and Michael Faraday were all poisoned by the chemicals they used in their experiments.

A nineteenth-century Scots inventor developed a twine-twisting machine which he intended to be powered by 10,000 mice.

Galileo blinded himself by looking at the sun through his telescope for too long.

The full name of the chemical tryptophan synthetase has 1,913 letters. Its formula is $C_{1289} H_{2051} N_{343} O_{375} S_8$.

An electric fan does not cool a room; it merely redistributes the air. And the heat generated by its motor makes the temperature of the air rise.

In 1753, Professor N. Kirchman was electrocuted by his attempt to draw 'electric flow' from the clouds.

* *Professor Beware* was a 1938 Harold Lloyd comedy. Lloyd, who had started life in Hollywood as an extra but was earning $40,000 a week by 1926, was the favourite performer of the deposed Emperor of China.

Bottoms Up

When the Luxembourg branch of Alcoholics Anonymous was founded in 1948, it had only two members.

Chinese babies do not wear nappies. They simply have a convenient hole cut in their trousers and are mopped up regularly.

King George II suffered from piles.

The first beer in cans came on to the market in 1935.

Four thousand years ago, the communities of the Indus valley had drains and lavatories. Yet when Versailles was built, there were no bathrooms or lavatories in the entire palace.

In 1743, one in six shops in London sold alcohol.

The first advert on commercial radio was for a laxative.

When the ancient Romans toasted a woman's health, they drank a glass of wine for every letter of her name.

Monkeys have tails which are obvious to the naked eye. Apes have no visible tails.

Napoleon's piles were so painful that he could not mount his horse to survey the field at the Battle of Waterloo, which may well have contributed to its loss.

Pubs were first licensed in 1551.

The eighteenth-century playwright Richard Brinsley Sheridan was a compulsive drinker who, for want of anything better, would drink eau-de-cologne.

The first modern British flush toilet was made for Queen Elizabeth I by John Harrington and cost 30s 8d.

A latrine built along Hadrian's Wall has room for 20 people to sit side by side.

Dry ginger ale boomed in popularity during Prohibition in the US because whisky could be added to it without changing the colour.

* Spencer Tracy didn't win an Oscar for his performance in *Bottoms Up* in 1934, but he shares with Marlon Brando, Fredric March and Gary Cooper the distinction of having won four 'Best Actor' awards.

Gentlemen Prefer Blondes

According to a recent survey, 68 per cent of men *do* prefer blondes. They think they're more fun and likely to be less intelligent than their darker sisters.

One thing was guaranteed to put Elvis Presley off a woman: big feet.

Thirteen per cent of American men would like to have sex more than once a day.

Over a period of forty-seven years, a man's heart will pump more than 300,000 tons of blood.

According to an Islamic sex manual recently published, husbands should not allow their women to go to the hairdresser or the beauty parlour or any other place where women gather, for fear of lesbianism.

A survey on male hygiene revealed that Japanese men use more anti-perspirants and deodorants than the males of any other nation. They even use more than Japanese women.

Men of the Tuareg tribes of the Sahara wear veils while their women go uncovered.

Males are twice as frequently left-handed as females. They are also more likely to fall out of bed.

Pericles, ruler of fifth-century Athens, was so self-conscious about his high forehead that he insisted on wearing a helmet for his portraits.

Although men think that a muscular chest is what attracts women, studies show that what really turns women on are men's buttocks.

The sight of women's feet aroused such lust in some Victorian men that photographers erased them from photos.

Tony Curtis, infuriated at being kept waiting for hours by Marilyn Monroe on the set of *Some Like It Hot*, declared that he would rather kiss Hitler than her.

Men are five times more likely than women to become alcoholics.

* In 1953, the year in which Marilyn Monroe starred in *Gentlemen Prefer Blondes*, a musical about two women in search of rich husbands, she was awarded the title of 'Best Newcomer of the Year.'

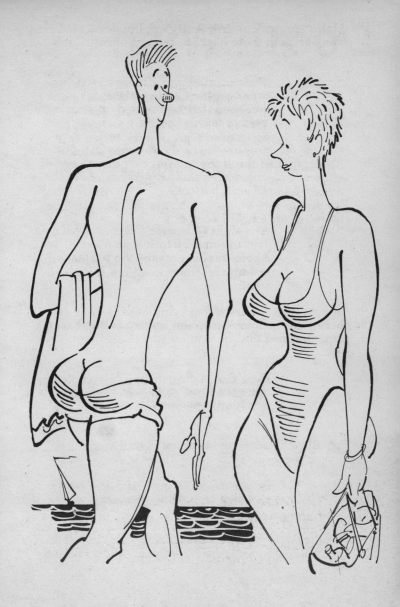

Death Wish

Fifty-eight thousand American men were killed during the Vietnam war, but it has been estimated that nearly twice that number have committed suicide since their return.

Despite the anti-smoking lobby, about nine million cigarettes are smoked each day.

Anyone caught stealing a Pekinese dog in Imperial times in China was put to death.

Having mated with the queen, the male bee dies; his penis breaks off.

More than twice as many psychologists commit suicide each year than do psychiatric patients in care.

In 1681, the dodo was last spotted on Mauritius.

Balzac drank 50 cups of coffee a day and died of caffeine poisoning.

Scientists have shown that snoring can kill. Many heavy snorers swallow their tongues, which can be fatal.

The most common cause of death in the age-group 20-30 is accidents.

Lord Lovat, the last man to be executed on Tower Hill scaffold, had the last laugh when a stand packed with ghoulish spectators collapsed, killing twelve of them.

Lightning kills more than 400 Americans each year.

The most vicious breed of dog, according to accident statistics, is the Alsatian. Number three on the list is the poodle.

Worldwide, about 1,000 people commit suicide on any given day.

The Earl of Morton was beheaded by the guillotine-style contraption he had himself introduced into Scotland.

At least ten countries have nuclear capacity to destroy the world.

* *Death Wish* was a great success for Charles Bronson in 1974. Around that time he was reported to be earning more than $20,000, plus $2,500 living allowance, each day.

F For Fake

Suet pudding, so long thought of as a classic English pudding, was introduced from Germany in 1715.

When the Mona Lisa was stolen in 1911, six Americans each paid $300,000 for what they were certain was the real thing.

Wooden money was produced and used in a Washington town in 1932 when the local bank folded and emergency currency was needed.

The Romans invented the sandwich and called it an 'offula' long before the Earl of Sandwich gave his name to it.

The Venezuelan cow tree produces sap that looks and tastes just like milk.

Captain Cook wasn't the European discoverer of Australia. At least three others had landed there before he did.

Marie Antoinette probably didn't say, 'Let them eat cake.' The saying, in various forms, was around long before then.

To avoid resentment in America about Japanese imports, the Japanese renamed one of their industrial areas USA so that they could legitimately stamp goods 'Made in USA'.

When Princess Margaret and Lord Snowdon were courting, they went under the aliases of Norman and Ruby Gordon.

Danish pastries do not come from Denmark.

More statues have been attributed to the Greek sculptor Praxiteles than he could have produced in his lifetime.

Although it has for a long time been believed that the guillotine was invented during the French Revolution by Dr Guillotin, a beheading machine was in use in Scotland in 1581 and similar contraptions were common in Italy.

6 *The last play I was ever in was* Next Time I'll Sing To You *which opened at the Arts Theatre. One night I heard a very distinctive laugh in the house and peered through the lights to see Orson Welles sitting in the stalls. At the time he was going to direct* The Bible *and after the show he came back to tell me, "I don't know what you're going to play, but you're going to be in* The Bible." *In the end John Huston directed it, but Orson and I have known each other ever since.*9

* True to its title, *F For Fake* wasn't what it appeared to be. It *looked* like a sophisticated lecture on life and truth, delivered by Orson Welles and illustrated in an arty fashion, but this 1973 French, West German and Iranian production consisted largely of documentaries no one could sell, chopped up in an impressive manner.

Something Big

There are more signal connections in the human brain than there would be in a telephone exchange connecting everyone on earth.

When an alligator bellows, the noise can be heard a mile away.

A South American fig tree has roots 120 metres (400 feet) beneath the surface of the soil. Its roots are longer than the height of any living tree.

The word *million* was first used in 1370.

The largest cheese in history was a Cheddar cheese 14 ft 6 in × 6 ft × 6 ft (4.4 metres long, 1.9 metres wide and 1.8 metres high). It weighed 17.5 tonnes.

At birth, a baby blue whale weighs about the same as a fully-grown hippopotamus.

The Crystal Palace, built for the Great Exhibition of 1851, was the largest single structure in the world and used a third of the annual British glass output.

Baby giraffes grow almost unbelievably quickly. A carefully measured giraffe born in 1937 grew more than 30 cm (12 inches) in a single day.

The largest Maori dug-out canoe was
35.7 metres (120 feet) long and carried
70 people.

The largest piece of space debris to fall to earth was
a one-tonne tank.

The largest book in the world is 7 ft tall
and 10 ft across (2.1 by 3 metres) when
open.

The Indonesian fruit bat has a wingspan larger
than that of most birds — 1.7 metres (5 ft 6 in).

Blue whales are at their heaviest in
January.

In Australia earthworms measuring 3.4 metres
(11 feet) have been discovered.

When Krakatoa exploded, the sound
was so loud that coastguards more
than 4,000 km (2,500 miles) away heard
the roar four hours after it happened.

* Dean Martin was the star of *Something
Big*, a semi-comic western released in
1971. Sadly, it wasn't as big as its
producers would have liked.

Chamber Of Horrors

When a Japanese gang leader was hacked to death in 1978, his assailants had to find a way of disposing of his fingerprints. They chopped off his hands and boiled them up to make soup, which they sold at a roadside stall.

In 1940, a man and three cows were burned to death in France for bestiality.

During the French Revolution, the skins of guillotined aristocrats were tanned to make leather, and one hide was used to bind the new French constitution.

Bird's nest soup, so popular in China, is made from the nest of the cave swiftlet. The bird uses its saliva to stick the nest together.

Mary Paterson, a beautiful Scots prostitute, was murdered by Burke and Hare and her body sold for dissection. But the doctor who bought it was so taken with his purchase that he kept her preserved in whisky for three months.

The Inquisition, started in the thirteenth century, was not abolished until 1834.

Sir Thomas More's daughter reclaimed his head after it had been parboiled and stuck on a pole on London Bridge for three months.

In the eighteenth century, teething babies were comforted by having a hare's brain rubbed on their gums.

Ines de Castro is probably the only queen to have been crowned after her death. She was exhumed, dressed and propped up on her throne for the occasion.

The American Food and Drug Administration sets stringent tests for food. For example, a 100 gram (3½ oz) sample of tomato purée must not contain more than thirty fly eggs. And it mustn't have a mould count of more than 40 per cent.

An eighteenth-century Indian was born with a headless 'twin' attached to his body so that he had two extra arms and legs.

* *Chamber of Horrors* (US 1960) was originally intended to be a TV movie but it turned out to be too scary. Tony Curtis, who was originally Bernard Schwarz, made a guest appearance.

Love Story

Czar Peter the Great had his mistress executed when he found she had been unfaithful, but he loved her all the same and kept her head preserved in a jar in his bedroom.

Snails kiss before mating.

To keep Louis XV's love, Madame de Pompadour lived on a diet of vanilla, truffles and celery — all of which were supposed to be aphrodisiacs.

Napoleon once bought Josephine a dress entirely covered in fresh rose petals.

Mills & Boon sell twenty million romantic novels each year in Great Britain.

Russian author Dostoyevsky was a foot fetishist. So was Scott Fitzgerald.

Male Adelie penguins present their chosen mate with a stone, which forms the basis of their nest. If she accepts, they stand chest to breast and sing a love song together.

The ancient Persians loved carpets so much, they wrote poems about the most beautiful ones.

Queen Victoria insisted that Albert's clothes were laid out every day — for forty years after his death.

When Lord Byron and Lady Caroline Lamb became lovers, they exchanged locks of pubic hair.

George IV wrote so many love letters to Mrs Fitzherbert that after his death they took two days to burn.

Jim Brady, a US railway millionaire, showed his love for actress Lillian Russell by buying her a gold-plated bicycle encrusted with precious jewels.

Mrs Martin van Butchell and her husband had more hate than love for each other. When she died, her will stated that her fortune be passed to a distant relative 'the moment I am dead and buried.' Mr van Butchell was so affronted that he refused to bury her. Her body was embalmed, dressed in finery, and she was displayed to the public every weekday in the drawing-room of their home.

* *Love Story* had its audiences weeping in the aisles in 1970 and made Ali McGraw a top box-office draw. Erich Segal, who wrote it, has said that a most important thing for romance is a sunset.

To Have And Have Not

Ten million vasectomies are performed each year so that men can have and have not.

James Dean, rebellious sex symbol, lost his front teeth at an early age and wore a special bridge with false ones. He used to take it out to deter his fans.

Rwanda in Central Africa has less than one telephone per thousand people.

Disposable sanitary protection is not available in Russia.

The kingdom of Saudi Arabia covers an area of 2,149,690 square kilometres (830,000 square miles), and there is not a single river in the entire country.

During his lifetime John Milton received just £10 for his masterpiece, *Paradise Lost.*

The Singer Company was the first to develop a hire-purchase scheme for people who wanted its sewing-machines.

Despite his great wealth, Farouk I, the last king of Egypt, was a petty thief.

On screen, Rudolph Valentino was the great lover —
but in real life his wife wasn't so keen on him and
their marriage was unconsummated.

The Museum of Modern Art in New
York had proudly displayed Matisse's
Le Bateau for nearly seven weeks
before someone noticed it was upside
down.

Seventy-five per cent of the liver can be removed and
the organ will continue to function normally, even
regenerating itself and returning to its original size.

Before he became king, George IV was
so poor and deep in debt that when his
carriage was held up by highwaymen
their haul amounted in today's terms to
only 15p.

‘ *As an actor who never let you see the machinery working
behind a part, Humphrey Bogart was one of my all-time
favourites. I got to know Lauren Bacall years later and then
found out everyone called her Betty.* ’

* **To Have And Have Not** (1945) was
the first film in which Humphrey Bogart
and Lauren Bacall were paired. They
enjoyed it so much that they decided to
stick together permanently.

Naughty
But Nice

In 1978 the first Indian film kiss
was allowed to be seen.

Yoko Ono once made a film entirely about bottoms.

Marilyn Monroe used to bleach her
pubic hair.

According to a Kinsey report, only 4 per cent of
married women frequently make love standing up.

Cesare Borgia's wedding night was
almost ruined by a joker who
substituted laxatives for the pills he
normally took.

France boasts towns called Arsy and Condom.

When men first competed naked in the
ancient Olympic Games, women were
banned from watching. Many,
however, gatecrashed in disguise.

In the film *Don Juan*, starring John Barrymore,
there is on average one kiss every 53 seconds.

Hedy Lamarr was an early star of nude
films and was the first actress to
participate in scenes of simulated sex.

Belly-dancing is one of the most widespread forms of entertainment in the world. It is popular in Hawaii, New Zealand and Africa, as well as Turkey.

Part of croquet's attraction for Victorians was the chance for gentlemen to glance at ladies' ankles as they played strokes.

The Page Three girl has been around for almost as long as newspapers. Eighteenth-century papers often contained daring semi-nudes based on classical paintings and statues.

In the film *Caligula* one of the orgy scenes was real.

When George Sand left her lover Alfred de Musset for another man, he got his revenge by writing a pornographic novel, *Gemiani*, about her.

❛ *Ronald Reagan's best film was* King's Row, *an opinion I'm not alone in holding. When Jane Wyman was asked why their marriage had ended in divorce, she is said to have replied, "Because I have to watch* King's Row *every night."* **❜**

* *Naughty But Nice* was made in 1939, so it isn't very naughty by modern standards. It does, however, feature Ronald Reagan in the days before he exchanged Hollywood for the White House.

Educating Rita

The most popular set book for 'O'
and 'A' level English Literature
exams is *Sons and Lovers* by D.H.
Lawrence.

Mozart, who was taught by his father, wrote his first
symphony at the age of eight and became a salaried
concertmaster at the age of eleven.

Sarah Bernhardt's talent for shocking
people began early; she was three times
suspended from school before she was
sixteen, once for spending an
unchaperoned evening with a soldier.

Princess Diana failed all five of her 'O' levels twice
in 1977.

Since the 1920s, the US government's
film-making agencies have made more
than 500 education films about teeth
and how to care for them.

The three terms at Oxford are known as Trinity,
Michaelmas and Hilary.

Mussolini was expelled from school
after stabbing a fellow pupil in the
buttocks.

Irving Berlin, America's most prolific songwriter,
never learned to read and write music.

Lord Byron's daughter was a brilliant mathematician who helped to invent the first computer.

In 1978, only 2 per cent of the population of Barking had a university degree. In the same year, 16.5 per of the population of Richmond-upon-Thames had degrees.

The philospher Epicurus was teaching female students in 300 BC.

Not so many years ago, a woman entertaining a man in her room at certain Cambridge colleges had either to be chaperoned or to put her bed in the corridor.

Senator Edward Kennedy was suspended from Harvard for cheating in exams.

Two out of three of the world's women are illiterate.

There is approximately one library book for each person on earth.

❝ *I developed my part in* Educating Rita *from a combination of a business partner whose dedication to the bottle is only matched by another close friend, Robert Bolt's, air of scholarship. Together they gave me the basis for my English professor, who was fleshed out (literally) by a tummy that I acquired with great pleasure, a shaggy beard, old clothes and a slightly reddened nose. We were filming in Trinity College, Dublin, and soon after starting I saw a man walking up to us looking exactly like a smaller version of me — beard, gut, nose and all. He was carrying a case of red wine. "I've read about you," he said to me, "you like wine. Come up and have a drop of this," showing me a very good Bordeaux. I looked closely at him, asked if he taught English, and when he said he did, I knew I'd got the part right!* ❞

It's a Mad Mad Mad Mad World

The 8th Earl of Bridgewater used to give lavish dinner parties for dogs. All his canine friends were dressed in the stylish silks and satins of the day and dined off silver.

Author Truman Capote wrote only on yellow paper.

The Japanese are so crazy about golf, they've blown the tops off mountains to make courses.

The first Romanian World Cup team was personally selected by King Carol.

The average British farm worker's labour produces £180,000 each year. The average farm worker is paid £5,500 pa.

Biro ink contains castor oil.

Although Rye is one of the Cinque Ports, it is more than a mile (1.6 km) from the sea.

False beards were all the rage in fourteenth-century Spain, and Peter the Great of Russia put a tax on real ones during his reign.

The phrase 'time immemorial' officially covers the period before the reign of Richard I.

There is a street in California named after a Chinese recluse. It's called Wong Way.

As well as Mother's Day and Father's Day the Americans celebrate Secretary's Day and Boss's Day.

On her trip to the Arabian Gulf in 1979, the Queen was presented with a solid gold chainmail pinafore.

The Maltese language is derived from Arabic, but is written in the Roman alphabet.

During one of his attacks of insanity, George III insisted on ending every sentence he uttered with the word *peacock*.

*   *It's a Mad Mad Mad Mad World*, made in 1963, has gone down in the annals of film history as the ultimate chase film. Unfortunately it suffered from too much of many good things — including a star cast of Spencer Tracy, Jimmy Durante, Ethel Merman, Phil Silvers, Jack Benny, Buster Keaton and Mickey Rooney.

Crime And Punishment

King Gustav III of Sweden believed coffee was poisonous, and once ordered a criminal to prove it by drinking himself to death. The condemned man survived to the age of 83.

The act permitting condemned criminals to be boiled to death was repealed in 1547.

For locking herself in the men's lavatory of the all-male Sparrow's Club after sneaking in disguised as a man, Mrs Frances Bird-Loughton was fined £25.

The 'human fly' who climbed the World Trade Center in 1977 was fined $1.10 for doing so.

According to the Koran, a woman who commits adultery should be stoned to death. However, if she is a slave and has not received a proper education, allowances are made.

Pope Alexander VI died after consuming poison he had intended for his cardinals.

In King Canute's day, adulterous women had their noses and ears cut off.

Painless childbirth was long opposed by churchmen on the grounds that the pains were part of women's punishment for Eve's sin in the Garden of Eden.

Witches who were tried by Bible were generally declared innocent. Both Bible and 'witch' were weighed, and if the accused weighed more than the Bible she was released.

In a judgment passed in 1837, it was decided that if a man kissed a woman against her will she was entitled to bite off his nose.

English pamphleteer William Prynne had his ears cut off for his inflammatory publications.

Male belly-dancing was outlawed in Egypt in 1837 because of the enthusiastic riots it caused. Belly-dancing boys were far more popular than female dancers.

It is illegal to hunt camels in Arizona.

* The 1935 film of Dostoyevsky's *Crime and Punishment* is, at best, heavy going. Undeterred by this, Marilyn Monroe wanted to make a film of another famous novel of Dostoyevsky's, *The Brothers Karamazov*.

Three Into Two Won't Go

French mathematicians have produced a 400-page book showing the value of π (pi), to one million figures.

A googol is the mathematical term for the number ten followed by one hundred zeros.

Minus 40°C is the same as minus 40°F.

The most common single-letter surname is O.

The average wink takes about one-tenth of a second.

The odds against being attacked by a shark are, fortunately, very long — 30,000,000 to 1.

The first = (equals sign) was used in an algebra text published in 1557.

The femtometre is the smallest unit of length. It is expressed as 10^{-15}m.

Trained 'noses' working in perfume factories are capable of distinguishing between 20,000 odours.

The earth travels more than 2,900,000 km (1,500,000 miles) every day.

There is 38.5 times as much salt water as fresh water on earth.

The average glass of London tap water has already been through a human body seven times.

There's no reason why a week should be seven days long. In ancient Mesopotamia a week was six days long and in West Africa four days. French revolutionaries tried to establish a ten-day week.

The earth would fit into the sun 109 times.

According to an expert hangman, a 75 kg (165 lb) man will require a drop of 2.6 metres (8 ft 6 in) for a clean death.

* *Three Into Two Won't Go* was a 1969 production, written by Edna O'Brien, about a *ménage à trois*. It starred Rod Steiger, Claire Bloom and Peggy Ashcroft who, after a long acting career, won her first Oscar in 1985 for *A Passage to India*.

Once In A Lifetime

Determined to look smart for her execution, Mata Hari had a special outfit made for the occasion.

Gary Cooper started his film career as a stunt man before being spotted and turned into a star.

For his historic solo flight across the Atlantic, Charles Lindbergh had a special fuel tank built on to the nose of his plane so that he wouldn't be crushed in a crash. This made visibility so difficult he had to use a periscope to see where he was going.

Because she was born on the day of Edward VIII's coronation, an Exeter woman was christened Coronation. Then she married a Mr Street — and became Coronation Street.

Shirley Williams was once considered for the starring role in *National Velvet*. Elizabeth Taylor got the part and became one of the world's biggest stars.

Paul Getty was the only man ever to knock out heavyweight champion Jack Dempsey.

In Bram Stoker's original novel, Dracula had a moustache. Only one Dracula film has shown him with one.

Thomas Jefferson, president of the US, invented the swivel chair.

The novelist Anthony Trollope invented pillar boxes.

Gilbert and Sullivan, famed for their comic operas, once wrote a bawdy piece called *The Sod's Opera*.

Before she became a screen goddess, Greta Garbo made a living giving manicures in a Stockholm barber shop.

In 1908, a horse that normally pulled a plough won the Grand National.

John Wayne started his film career as a prop man at Fox's studios.

White Cloud, friend of Sitting Bull and chief of the Red Indian Creek nation, had a change of life and became a spiritualist healer and patent medicine salesman.

* *Once in a Lifetime* (US 1933) was one of Hollywood's first satires about itself. Unfortunately, the people of Afghanistan were not able to appreciate it. The first cinema to open there arrived in 1939.

Change Of Mind

In 1850, Henry Wells and William Fargo started a business — called American Express. Two years later they changed the name to Wells-Fargo.

Laura Bell was London's most expensive prostitute before she had a change of mind, married a bishop and became a preacher.

Sherlock Holmes was blacklisted in Russia because of his belief in spiritualism. However, the authorities have changed their minds and Sir Arthur Conan Doyle's stories can once more be read in the USSR.

If any of his stars tried to rebel against him, Louis B. Mayer would cry until they changed their minds.

In 1962, Robert Wagner and Natalie Wood were divorced. Ten years later they changed their minds and married again.

Jane Austen originally intended to call *Northanger Abbey* by another title — *Susan*.

Because the literal translation of 'grease' means 'fat' in Spanish, promoters changed their minds about using it. Instead, *Grease* appeared in Venezuela as *Vaseline*.

Sir John Popham, who became a sixteenth-century Chief Justice of England, started his life as a burglar.

Dustin Hoffman got his break in *The Graduate* after Robert Redford turned the role down. Maybe Redford should have changed his mind.

Catch 22 was originally entitled *Catch 18*.

For the first years of his career, Stevie Wonder was promoted as 'Little Stevie Wonder'. Then he grew to be six feet tall.

The 1925 British film was released as *Livingstone* in its home country but as *Stanley* in the US.

According to statistics, the average Swedish man regularly buys five different pornographic magazines — but he won't be allowed to for much longer. After the liberalisation of the 60s, many Swedes want a return to censorship.

* *Change of Mind* was a 1969 story about a brain transplant. Despite its sensational topic, it managed to be dull.

Stage Struck

The menstrual cycles of MGM's actresses were carefully plotted on charts so that filming schedules could be planned around them.

A magician called Chung Lin Soo was literally stage struck at the Empire Theatre in north London when his 'bullet-catching' trick went disastrously wrong. He dropped dead in front of his audience.

Ballerinas have to use as many as three pairs of shoes for a single ballet because they wear out so quickly.

One of the strangest stage acts ever seen was the Amazing Regurgitator, a man who swallowed a number of objects and then regurgitated a specific item at the request of the audience.

Charles Dickens used to work himelf up to such a pitch when he performed his own work on stage that he sometimes fainted.

William Ireland forged a new version of *King Lear* and various documents supposed to have been written by Shakespeare. He surpassed himself when he wrote *Voltigern*, which he claimed was a lost Shakespearian play. Scholars examined it and pronounced it authentic, but when it was performed it was so awful it was booed off.

The poster advertising *Casablanca* is the best-selling poster of all time.

While he was Prince of Wales, Edward VII appeared for a single performance of *Fedora* opposite Sarah Bernhardt.

Hamlet is the longest Shakespearian role.

The pantomime as we know it first started in 1860 with *Cinderella*, a 'Fairy Burlesque'.

The first can-can to be danced on an English stage was seen in 1866.

Actors gather at the Drury Lane Theatre on Twelfth Night to cut the Baddeley cake and drink punch. The cake and punch are supplied under the terms of Robert Baddeley's will.

Covent Garden tube station is haunted by a Victorian actor.

In *Julius Caesar*, Shakespeare makes reference to a clock striking. Clocks didn't appear until a thousand years after Caesar's death.

*   *Stage Struck* (1936) was a less than spectacular musical starring Dick Powell and Joan Blondell. When Dick Powell wanted to marry an MGM actress called June Allyson, he was opposed by Louis B. Mayer himself. Mayer didn't think Powell was famous enough for his protégée.

Never Too Late

In 1963, Françoise Gilot left her long-time lover Pablo Picasso because he was continually unfaithful — by then Picasso was in his eighties.

The Duke of Wellington began his last affair at the age of 83.

The *New York Times* published an apology to a professor 49 years after his theories about space travel, which they had scoffed at, were proved correct.

Evangelist Aimee Semple McPherson was buried with a telephone in her coffin so that she could contact the living world. After seven years without a call from her, the line was disconnected.

El Cid won a battle when he was dead. His embalmed body was strapped to a horse and sent out on to the battlefield to rally his troops at a critical moment.

Elizabeth Barrett Browning, Rose Kennedy and Audrey Hepburn all had children after the age of forty.

There is no upper age limit for MPs.

Catherine the Great took a 22-year-old lover when she was 60.

W.B. Yeats took up fencing at the age of 45.

The King of Tonga used to be required to deflower every virgin on the island, and was still performing his duties eight times a week at the age of 80.

Anne Hathaway, Isadora Duncan and Catherine of Aragon all married men younger than themselves.

Winston Churchill wrote *A History of the English-Speaking Peoples* at the age of 82.

The world's first crossword puzzle appeared in 1913, but the *New York Times* held out until 1950 before publishing one.

For anyone who lives to the age of 105, there is the reward of a telegram from the Queen on every birthday.

* In 1965 Maureen O'Sullivan starred in *Never Too Late*, a story about a middle-aged housewife who discovers that she is pregnant. Just four years later, a South African grandmother had a baby at the age of 58.

The Odd Couple

When King Farouk of Egypt
abdicated, he went to stay with
Gracie Fields in Capri.

Both David Bowie and Elton John have admitted to
being bisexual.

Anne Bonney and Mary Read were
eighteenth-century pirates who wore
men's clothing and fought alongside
their men. When they were caught,
they escaped the death sentence
because, unlike most pirates, they were
able to claim that they were pregnant.

Richard Wagner lived with his wife and two
mistresses, all of them acknowledging one another.

Miles Darden's top weight was 460 kg
(1,020 lb). His wife weighed a mere
44 kg (98 lb).

The duck-billed platypus and the spiny anteater are
the world's only egg-laying mammals.

Eva Peron and Aristotle Onassis once
had an affair. They must have made
an intriguing couple.

New York has fourteen exclusively gay cinemas.

Twins have been born forty-eight days apart in the US.

Prince Liu Sheng, a second-century Chinese ruler, and his wife were buried in jade funeral suits consisting of more than 2,000 interlinked tiles. The suits were supposed to prevent the decomposition of their bodies.

Sea bass are female until their fifth year, when many of them become male.

One of Queen Victoria's presents to her husband Albert was a solid silver lunchbox in which to carry his sandwiches — though why Prince Albert needed to carry sandwiches is something of a mystery. ●

Elsa Lanchester was so shocked by Charles Laughton's confession of his homosexuality that she went deaf for a week.

❝ Walter Matthau has one line for me. Every time I see him he says, "Hello Michael, still in show business?" ❞

* In 1968 *The Odd Couple* paired Jack Lemmon, who was at the time the fourth-biggest box office draw in the US, and Walter Matthau in a Neil Simon comedy. The result was a great success.

Superman

Ghengis Khan conquered more territory during his lifetime than any other leader.

Rex Harrison has only one eye.

President William Taft of the US was so fat that a special bathtub had to be made for him in which four workmen could sit in comfort.

A British soldier walked non-stop for 6 days, 10 hours and 22 minutes.

Mormon leader Brigham Young had 56 children.

Barry Manilow achieved the fastest ever sell-out on Broadway.

Indian poet Sri Chinmoy composed 843 poems in a single day in 1975.

John Dillinger robbed more banks in a single year than Jesse James did in sixteen.

In 1972 and 1973 a poll at Madame Tussaud's revealed that Richard Nixon was hated more than Adolf Hitler.

Rasputin's penis, which was cut off when he was killed, was preserved in a case made specially for it. The case measured 45 cm by 15 cm (18 in × 6 in).

Charlie Chaplin insured his feet for $150,000.

An Englishman is currently trying to circumnavigate the globe on a diet of dehydrated dog food.

St Simeon the Younger spent 45 years sitting on top of a pole in Syria.

While researching material for his book *Sexual Behaviour and the Human Male*, Alfred Kinsey discovered the case of a man who'd had more than five sexual encounters each day for a period of thirty years.

The Cerne Abbas Giant, a huge male figure carved into the chalk hillside in Dorset, is 900 times larger than life.

* *Superman*, a joint British and American production in 1978, may be the most expensive movie ever made. Estimated cost was $55 million. Marlon Brando, who appeared for a mere ten minutes as Superman's father, received $3 million for his performance — and then sued successfully for a further $15 million, which he felt was his share of the gross profits. His total of $18 million for a ten-minute role is unlikely to be beaten for a long time.

Boom!

In 1956, an American architect put forward a proposal for nuclear-powered lifts in his skyscraper.

Ordinary yeast was used in the manufacture of high explosives in World War I.

A stadium costing $840,000 was built for the Tokyo Olympic Games. It was used for four days and demolished a year later for a new development.

Leonardo da Vinci invented the parachute in 1480. Unfortunately, no one found a use for it for nearly 400 years.

In *The Winter's Tale*, Shakespeare writes about a shipwreck on the coast of Bohemia. Bohemia has no coastline.

On seeing the first rushes of Laurence Olivier in *Wuthering Heights*, Sam Goldwyn called him, '...a mess, dirty, unkempt, stagey, hammy and awful.' Olivier got an Oscar nomination for his performance.

The average person in the US Virgin Islands uses more supplied energy in a single day than the average person in Kampuchea uses in 62 years.

Soya beans are used in the manufacture of paint, glue, plastics — and explosives.

California is the largest prune-producing area in the world.

To demonstrate its safety, Arnold Bennett drank a glass of tap water while in Paris in 1931. He contracted typhoid fever from it and died.

Octopuses and squid are jet-propelled.

Archaeological finds in Iraq suggest that primitive electrical batteries may have been in use there 2,000 years ago.

The human race doubles in number approximately every thirty-five years.

Modern books have a life expectancy of only 100 years, because the sulphuric acid in wood-pulp paper rots rapidly.

❛ *Elizabeth Taylor and I made* Zee & Co. *Now she's not very tall and I'm six feet two, so when we shot any scenes close together, she stood on a box. I used to tell her that everyone would think I was only an inch taller than her, adding, "I'm going to look like Mickey Rooney leaving* Boy's Town*" — and ever since she's called me "Little Mickey".* ❜

* *Boom!* was a notorious 1968 flop, despite the combined talents of Richard Burton, Elizabeth Taylor and Noel Coward. Coward must have looked back nostalgically to the days in 1942 when he had written, directed and acted in *In Which We Serve.*

Bringing Up Baby

Turkeys are particularly prone to virgin birth.

Legend has it that Gorgias, an ancient Greek, was born in the coffin in which his mother lay dead.

Queen Anne had seventeen children, none of whom survived her.

It used to be the custom to pass a newly-born child through the rind of a cheese.

The Greeks believed that sex while a north wind was blowing would produce a male baby. A southern wind was supposed to result in a female child.

The baby blue whale takes only two years to reach maturity. No other animal grows as quickly.

In 1970, a German mother gave birth to twins — one white and one black.

In the 1850s, the average couple had six children.

At the age of three Henry VI opened Parliament and cried throughout the ceremony.

In 1975, the most popular names for new babies in Australia were Matthew and Michelle.

Babies have more bones than adults.
As they grow, many bones join to form
a single one.

Baby whales are born tail first.

Baby shrews are led around in
procession by their mother, each
gripping the tail of the shrew in front.

Toys on wheels, just like those children pull along
today, were being made in Persia more than 2,000
years ago.

The Chinook Indians think a flat skull
is beautiful, and so for the first year
their babies' heads are strapped to a
piece of board to make them flat.

The hamster carries its babies for just sixteen days.
The female African elephant is pregnant for 640
days.

* *Bringing Up Baby*, starring Cary Grant
and Katharine Hepburn, was one of the big
successes of 1938. Hepburn was more
famously teamed with Spencer Tracy, with
whom she appeared nine times.

O Lucky Man

Vic Pollard of New Zealand was
offered places in his nation's World
Cup and cricket squads. He decided
to play cricket.

In 1757, the Prince de Condé made love twelve times
in a single night. To celebrate this event he had his
shirts, buttons and accessories marked with the
figure twelve.

Until the twentieth century, Egyptian
men did not like the job of deflowering
their new brides. They generally paid a
servant to do it for them.

Any man unlucky enough to be castrated can
console himself with one thought; castration is the
only proven way to prevent hair loss.

In 1857, Queen Victoria's rat catcher
earned more than her poet laureate,
Alfred, Lord Tennyson.

Charlie Chaplin was the first star to be signed for a
million dollars.

James Bartley was swallowed by a
whale in 1891 and stayed inside its
stomach for two days. He survived and
lived until 1926.

President Jimmy Carter was an honorary member of
Errol Flynn's fan club.

Contrary to popular belief, Thomas Crapper did not invent the WC.

Henry VIII wore skirts.

William Shakespeare's signature, of which there are only seven known specimens, is estimated to be worth about $1.5 million.

1,100 bald men found themselves in demand when Fritz Lang made *Metropolis* in 1926.

A man with a wooden leg was employed to ride up and down the newly-installed escalators at Earls Court station to give other travellers confidence.

The creator of the aerosol spray has made more than $100 million.

*   Malcolm McDowell's early career as a coffee salesman came in useful when he starred in *O Lucky Man* in 1973 — as a coffee salesman. He probably didn't have the same first-hand experience when it came to tackling the title role in that softporn extravaganza, *Caligula*. When he was Roman Emperor Caligula had a bed made to accommodate himself, his wife, his sister, a dozen female slaves — and his horse.

The Agony And The Ecstasy

King Charles VII of France was so terrified of being poisoned that he starved himself to death.

To keep herself slim, Faye Dunaway has only one meal a day.

The Pacific island of Nauru is so packed with minerals that when they've all been mined, only a fifth of the island will be left.

At the age of seventy, Lord Salisbury developed a passion for tricycling. He employed a servant to push him up hills; on the descent the servant was allowed to coast down perched on the back axle.

The man who wrote 'Pack up your troubles in your old kit bag and smile, smile, smile' committed suicide.

Heroin addiction causes constipation.

Queen Elizabeth I rarely ate a hot meal, so far were the kitchens from her banqueting hall.

The excised organs of Chinese eunuchs were preserved in alcohol, so that when they died their bodies could be buried in entirety.

Werewolves and vampires may well have existed. People who suffer from an agonising condition called *porphyria* become exceptionally sensitive to light, lose their noses and fingers — which gives them an animal look — and become hairy. Their teeth also become prominent. Modern sufferers are treated with a substance extracted from blood; past victims may have tried to relieve their pain by drinking blood.

Though the average modern American has a more active sex life than his predecessors, his sperm count is less than 50 per cent of what it was 50 years ago. In fact he's half the man he used to be.

The comfort of partitioned public loos was first available at the Great Exhibition of 1851. Entrance was a penny — hence the phrase 'spending a penny'.

Winston Churchill suffered so badly from depression that he did not allow himself to stand at the edge of railway platforms in case he jumped under a train.

* *The Agony and the Ecstasy*, which was about Michaelangelo's interior decoration of the Sistine Chapel, was a heavy-going 1965 drama starring Rex Harrison and Charlton Heston. Rex Harrison starred in *Doctor Dolittle* in 1967. This film lost a great deal of money, partly because of its cast of animals, which could not be guaranteed to perform on cue. At one point, ducks were turned loose on a pond; they sank like stones because it was the moulting season and they had lost their waterproof feathers.

The Talk Of
The Town

More than 13,000 existing towns and cities can claim to have been mentioned in the Domesday Book.

The first British pavements were laid in Edinburgh in 1688.

Birmingham was once described as the toy shop of Europe.

The first English daily paper was the *Daily Courant*, started in 1702.

The mechanical semaphore system established in France in the nineteenth century allowed a message to be sent 125 miles across country in three minutes.

Only one word of dialogue is spoken in Mel Brook's film *Silent Movie*.

At the turn of the century, an American woman developed a peculiar obsession; she believed that the day she stopped building work on her house would be the day she died. Neighbours watched as the house was extended over the years to cover six acres. Then one day there was a building strike. On that day the obsessive builder died.

The last English town to become a city was Derby.

In the eighteenth century, the macaroni inspired a great deal of talk. No, people weren't discussing pasta — a macaroni was a young dandy who dressed and behaved in the latest foppish fashion.

The first athletic events can be traced back to ancient Egypt, where there is evidence of organised races around the city walls of Memphis.

The first shoes with heels appeared in 1595 and caused a sensation.

The royal family was the talk of the town in 1893 when Queen Victoria, Princess Alexandra and the Prince of Wales all entered their dogs for Crufts.

In 1937, the *Washington Daily News* became the first paper to use a perfumed page — which must have caused some excitement over breakfast.

* Cary Grant, Ronald Colman and Jean Arthur were the stars of *The Talk of the Town*, released in 1942. Cary Grant had the unusual experience of playing himself in *Without Reservations*.

Summer Holiday

In 1983, 43 per cent of British adults did not have a holiday away from home.

The Queen always travels with a hot water bottle and a white kid lavatory seat.

Pilgrims going to Mecca must not clip their nails, raise their voices, cut their hair or have sex.

Between July and September 1982, almost 600 million days out were taken by adults and children in Britain.

Thomas Cook was the first travel agent to offer packaged continental holidays.

William Beckford travelled Europe in the eighteenth century escorted by his doctor, baker, cook, three footmen, a valet and twenty-four musicians. At every place he stopped, a room had to be specially decorated for him.

Eric the Red encouraged the first tourism by christening the vast ice-covered island he discovered Greenland — and trying to get people to go there. Iceland, where Eric came from, is *not* covered in ice.

All females are barred from the monastery of Mount Athos in Greece — and that includes animals.

When the first World Cup competition was held in Uruguay in 1930, only four European countries sent their teams on the three-week boat trip to South America.

Freud could never work out railway timetables, so he always took a companion when he travelled.

In 1974, more people went to East Germany for a holiday than to Greece.

On the island of Tahiti, tipping is thought to be a disgusting custom.

It is still possible to travel from London to Hong Kong by train.

The Romans invented the bikini.

* Cliff Richard starred in *Summer Holiday* in 1962 — and more than twenty years later he looks barely a day older!

The Stars
Look Down

Mercury has a day twice as long as
its year. It takes 88 days for
Mercury to revolve around the sun,
which gives it an 88-day year. But
it revolves on its axis only once
every 176 days.

Jupiter has a day that lasts just 9 hours and 50
minutes.

A satellite launched in the 1970s
showed that the Amazon had been
incorrectly charted on maps.

Though scientists talk confidently about black holes,
not one has ever been seen.

Because of the time it takes for light to
reach the earth, the sun has been up
for about eight minutes before we
actually see it.

Andromeda is the galaxy nearest our own.

Pluto's single moon moves at the same
rate as the planet itself revolves. This
means that anyone living on Pluto
would always see the moon in the same
place. For anyone on the other side of
the planet the moon would never
appear.

The moon is older than the earth, with the oldest moon rock dating back 5.3 billion years in comparison to earth's 3.7 billion years.

Mark Twain was born when Halley's Comet appeared in 1835, and died the next time it appeared in 1910.

The coldest place on earth, in Antarctica, has an average temperature warmer than the daytime temperature on Mars.

The earth spins faster in September than it does in March.

Pluto is so far away that if it were possible to stand on it the sun would appear only as bright as Venus does from the earth.

Blue and red moons appear relatively frequently due to dust in the atmosphere. But only twice has a green moon been seen.

* *The Stars Look Down* was a 1939 British social drama starring Michael Redgrave and Margaret Lockwood. The Redgrave family hold the record for the most generations of screen actors in a family.

The Swarm

In India, Africa and Brazil, wounds are sometimes closed by allowing termites to bite through the edges. The powerful jaws act like a modern surgical clip and stay in place when the insects' bodies are broken off.

The water spider lives underwater and breathes by trapping a bubble of air on its body and carrying it back to its nest.

One favoured form of Roman execution was stinging to death. The condemned were covered with honey and voracious wasps were let loose on them.

Cicadas vibrate their bodies 500 times a second.

Some ant societies are based on slavery. Grubs are captured and when the young ants hatch into adults they are put to work.

Carpet beetles trapped in bottles can live for two years with nothing to feed on but their own skins.

When it gets cold, bees congregate around their honeycombs and shiver. The motion heats up the hive.

There are probably more than a million species of insect on earth.

If you weighed all the world's insects against all the other animals on the planet, the insects would be heavier.

Queen termites live for up to fifty years — and lay one egg per second in that time.

Bees communicate with one another by using an elaborate system of tail-wagging and whirling. But they don't all 'speak' the same language: German and Egyptian bees cannot understand one another.

Earwigs are so called because it used to be believed that they liked entering the human ear.

❝ *Something I learned making* The Swarm *is that bees do not foul their own habitation. We needed thousands of bees for this film (the US was supposed to be under threat from them) and they were all cooped up until we started shooting. Once free though, they relieved themselves promptly and I kept finding my white laboratory coat covered in little brown spots. "That's bee shit, kid," the bee keeper explained when I asked him — prophetic some might say, judging by the reception the film got!* ❞

* *The Swarm*, made in 1978, was an all-star disaster movie that proved to be a disaster in all ways.

The Dirty Dozen

The first issue of *The Lady* gave readers detailed instructions on how to take a bath — but the article was illustrated with pictures of a man for propriety's sake.

Carl Stommfelder spent the last years of his life living in a bath. He ate, slept and conducted his business from his tub, and asked to be buried in it.

During the mating season, male squirrel monkeys develop disgusting habits, including urinating in each other's faces.

Many Welsh miners used not to wash their backs because they believed that it would weaken their backs.

Karl Marx rarely bathed and was plagued with boils for many years.

Far from being dirty, Clark Gable was obsessive about keeping clean and used to shave off his chest hair.

King Louis XIII took five baths in his life, and all of them unwillingly.

Peruvian Indians wash their babies in llama urine to ward off evil spirits.

The men who used to clean out cesspits were known as gongfermers.

Tibetans grow their left-hand little fingernails so that they can clean out their ears and noses efficiently.

To keep themselves warm, Tibetans traditionally rub themselves with rancid yak fat.

When dye was added to the soap used by nurses in an operating theatre, 50 per cent of them were shown not to have washed parts of their thumbs.

In 1974, people in Great Britain bought more soap per head than any other European country.

The Romans used sponges held on sticks and dipped into water instead of toilet paper.

*   *The Dirty Dozen*, a US/Spanish co-production of 1967, was a slick and successful story of twelve convicts sent on a suicide mission. In starred Lee Marvin, Ernest Borgnine, Charles Bronson, John Cassavetes and Donald Sutherland.

A Christmas Carol

In 1649, Oliver Cromwell abolished Christmas and declared that it was to be an ordinary working day. People who celebrated as usual were arrested.

The carol 'Silent Night' was written to be accompanied by a single guitar when the organ in a German church broke down.

In 1983, it was estimated that the cost of the gifts in the song 'The Twelve Days of Christmas' would total £6,277.20p.

The turkey was first imported to France by the Jesuits and it is still known in some French dialects as a *jésuite*.

In the nineteenth century, the Post Office used to deliver cards on Christmas morning.

Father Christmas lives in Edinburgh *and* the North Pole. Letters addressed to Toyland or Snowland go to Edinburgh, but letters addressed to the North Pole have to be sent there because there is such a place.

The first special Christmas stamp was printed by the Canadians in 1898.

Sir Isaac Newton, Humphrey Bogart and Princess Alexandra were all born on Christmas Day.

It's not until Twelfth Night, or the Feast of the Epiphany, that the figures of the Three Kings are added to the Christmas crib. Twelfth Night is known in German as 'Three Kings Day.'

Christmas crackers were invented by Thomas Smith, who had imported some French novelties as Christmas gifts. Unfortunately they weren't selling well — until he wrapped them up and gave them a 'bang'.

The royal family exchange Christmas presents on Christmas Eve.

An old tradition says that bread baked on Christmas Eve will never go mouldy.

W.C. Fields and Charlie Chaplin both died on Christmas Day.

The very first Christmas pudding was a kind of soup with raisins and wine in it.

* *A Christmas Carol*, from the story by Charles Dickens, was made by MGM in 1938. Dickens knew London intimately and often received inspiration for his novels while walking as many as twenty miles a night around the city in an attempt to cure his insomnia.

Those Were The Days

Performances of *King Lear*, Shakespear's play about a mad king, were banned for thirty-two years during the reign of George III because of his obvious insanity.

The average lifespan of a caveman was eighteen years.

When cellophane first appeared, it was so expensive it was used to wrap only the most costly gifts.

The first public telephone kiosk was set up in Nottingham in 1908.

During the eighteenth century, the average consumption of sugar rose by fifteen times, most of it incorporated in tea, coffee and chocolate, which had all been recently introduced.

Preston North End was the first football club to win both the FA and league trophies.

Many people wondered what had happened to George I's wife, but during his lifetime no explanation for her absence was offered. In fact she was imprisoned in Germany for more than thirty years because she had dared to divorce him for adultery.

Goal nets were first introduced at a football match in Nottingham in 1891.

When a Danish author wrote a book criticising the Swedes, who were at that time occupying Denmark, he was given the choice of being beheaded or of eating his own words. He ate his words by boiling the book in broth and making soup.

In 1272, a Bible in nine handwritten volumes cost around £33.

The Egyptians had established a calendar of 360-day years and twelve 30-day months as early as 4000 BC.

In France in 1740, a cow was found guilty of sorcery and hanged.

The last year to contain a 30 February was 11BC. After that, Augustus Caesar reorganised the calendar.

*   Although *Those Were the Days* (1934) starring Will Hay and John Mills, didn't set the world alight, its background of the old-time music hall is historically very interesting.

The End

Napoleon's stomach ended up in a silver pepper pot and his shrivelled, one-inch penis on sale at a London auction room — where its failure to reach a reserve price must have been the most final of indignities.

Before Queen Victoria's funeral it was customary for royals to be buried without pomp at night. She, however, made plans in her will for a state funeral.

To promote the wool trade, James I issued an order that everyone should be buried in a woollen shroud.

A Norfolk man laughed himself to death while watching an episode of *The Goodies*. His wife wrote to the comedy trio and thanked them for making his end such a happy one.

The last known castrato singer died in 1922.

Framas Ford Coppola had four different endings for his film *Apocalypse Now*. In the end he settled for just two of them, one for the 35 mm version and another for the 70 mm.

The last American member of the Bonaparte family died after tripping over a dog lead in Central Park.

The wild boar became extinct in Britain in 1683.

Madagascar was once the home of the elephant bird, believed by experts to have been 3 m (10 ft) tall and to have laid eggs seven times larger than those of the ostrich.

In 1956 more people crossed the Atlantic by ship than by plane — for the last time. It signalled the end of an era for the great liners.

The last pure-blooded Tasmanian died in 1876.

The ancient Britons practised euthanasia by jumping off rocks — or being pushed if they were too elderly to jump.

Nelson's coffin, situated in the crypt of St Paul's is made from the mast of a captured French ship. The black marble tomb surrounding it was originally intended as the resting-place of Cardinal Wolsey, one of Henry VIII's cardinals. Unfortunately, Wolsey fell out of favour and it was not used — until Nelson came along.

* *The End,* made in the US in 1978 and directed by and starring Burt Reynolds, really *was* the end as far as some of the critics were concerned. 'Tasteless ham,' was one of the kinder responses.

The National Playing Fields Association

The National Playing Fields Association is an independent charity with a Royal Charter devoted to the preservation, improvement and acquisition of playing fields, playgrounds and play space where they are most needed and for those who need them most, in particular children, young people and the handicapped.

When the Association was founded, back in 1925, land was relatively easy to obtain. Today the demand for land is creating a dangerous and growing threat to recreational spaces of all sorts. It is a threat the National Playing Fields Association is here to resist.

Every year some 11,500 children are fatally or seriously injured and approximately 500 children are killed in road accidents. Children and young people depend on adults to provide play and recreational opportunities and they are being let down. The National Playing Fields Association recognises that play is vital to a child's development. A child who cannot play is seriously deprived.

The charity's main concern has always been with the recreational needs of children and young people. How important are these? In positive terms, proper provision for children is basic to their healthy development. Lack of play and safe recreational opportunities can only lead to: loneliness, frustration, boredom, vandalism and crime.

After sixty years this message taken from the first page of the first Annual Report of the National Playing Fields Association still applies: 'The keeping of very small children off the streets by providing for them in congested areas small playgrounds where there is no risk of injury by motor or other wheeled traffic; and secondly, the provision of adequate playing fields for the masses of young people who, having no room themselves to play rush in thousands to look on at others playing, or perhaps indulge in less desirable pursuits.'

What does the charity do today?

It safeguards and maintains its own and other recreational land in its care — around one thousand fields, playgrounds and playing spaces in all.

It resists the loss of recreational land and stimulates and supports local initiatives to help save land that is under threat.

It purchases and helps to purchase recreational land for the benefit of the community as a whole.

It presses for wider acceptance of the official National Playing Fields Association Playing Space Target — the aim being six acres of usable playing space per thousand head of population.

It tests and organises research into safe and imaginative playing equipment and initiates innovative schemes, especially in the field of children's play.

If you would like to know more about the charity's work please write to:

THE NATIONAL PLAYING FIELDS ASSOCIATION
25, Ovington Square
London SW3 1LQ

THANK YOU!

Not many people know how indebted the National Playing Fields Association is to Michael Caine. In 1983 the Royal Premiere of *Educating Rita* brought some £13,000 to our Children's Play Appeal. In 1984 the charity got to know Michael Caine on a more personal basis when he took up our suggestion of publishing a book featuring some of the amazing (and amusing) bits of unusual information he has collected over the years. Because the book was an immediate success and rocketed to the top of the bestseller list, and because Mr Caine made sure that every penny of the royalties came to the charity, *Not Many People Know That* brought the Association an instant £30,000 with the promise of more to come. Not many people know that!